THE MANIPULATED MAN
is the most uncompromising challenge
yet hurled at women—by a woman!

"At a time when men are nervously scrutinizing
themselves for telltale signs of male chauvinism,
along comes Esther Vilar to take them under her
wing . . . Her descriptions of male and female
behavior are . . . wincingly accurate."
—*Oui* Magazine

The
Manipulated Man

Esther Vilar

BANTAM BOOKS · TORONTO · NEW YORK · LONDON

*This low-priced Bantam Book
has been completely reset in a type face
designed for easy reading, and was printed
from new plates. It contains the complete
text of the original hard-cover edition.*
NOT ONE WORD HAS BEEN OMITTED.

🚩

THE MANIPULATED MAN

*A Bantam Book / published by arrangement with
Farrar, Straus and Giroux, Inc.*

PRINTING HISTORY

*Farrar, Straus edition published November 1972
2nd printing .... December 1972
3rd printing .... February 1973
4th printing .... March 1973
Literary Guild edition published January 1973
Bantam edition published February 1974*

*This English version is based in part on a translation by Eva
Borneman, © 1972 by Abelard-Schuman Limited, and incor-
porates a new chapter, "American Man—the Most Successfully
Manipulated Male on Earth," translated by Ursula Bender, as
well as revisions by the author and other editorial changes based
on the original German book, Der dressierte Mann, © 1971 by
Esther Vilar.*

*Bantam Books are published by Bantam Books, Inc. Its trade-
mark, consisting of the words "Bantam Books" and the por-
trayal of a bantam, is registered in the United States Patent
Office and in other countries. Marca Registrada. Bantam
Books, Inc., 666 Fifth Avenue, New York, New York 10019.*

PRINTED IN THE UNITED STATES OF AMERICA

This book is dedicated to all those whom it does not mention: to the few men who refuse to be manipulated, to the few women who are not venal, and to all those fortunate enough to have lost their market value because they are either too old, too ugly, or too ill.

E.V.

Contents

The Slave's Happiness

THE LEMON-COLORED MG skids across the road, and the woman driver brings it to a somewhat uncertain halt. She gets out and finds her left front tire flat. Without wasting a moment she prepares to fix it: she looks toward the passing cars as if expecting someone. Recognizing this standard international sign of woman in distress ("weak female let down by male technology"), a station wagon draws up. The driver sees what is wrong at a glance and says comfortingly, "Don't worry. We'll fix that in a jiffy." To prove his determination, he asks for her jack. He does not ask if she is capable of changing the tire herself because he knows—she is about thirty, smartly dressed and made-up—that she is not. Since she cannot find her jack, he fetches his own, together with his other tools. Five minutes later the job is done and the punctured tire properly stowed. His hands are covered with grease. She offers him an embroidered handkerchief, which he politely refuses. He has a rag for such occasions in his tool box. The woman thanks him profusely, apologizing for her "typically feminine" helplessness. She might have been there till dusk, she says, had he not stopped. He makes no reply and, as she gets back into the car, gallantly shuts the door for her. Through the wound-down window he advises her to have her tire patched at once and she promises to get her garage man to see to it that very evening. Then she drives off.

As the man collects his tools and goes back to his own car, he wishes he could wash his hands. His shoes—he has been standing in the mud while changing the tire—are not as clean as they should be (he is a salesman). What is more, he will have to hurry to keep his next appointment. As he starts the engine he thinks, Women! One's more stupid than the next. He wonders what she would have done if he had not been there to help. He puts his foot on the accelerator and drives off—faster than usual. There is the delay to make up. After a while he starts to hum to himself. In a way, he is happy.

Almost any man would have behaved in the same manner—and so would most women. Without thinking, simply because men are men and women so different from them, a woman will make use of a man whenever there is an opportunity. What else could the woman have done when her car broke down? She has been taught to get a man to help. Thanks to his knowledge, he was able to change the tire quickly—and at no cost to herself. True, he ruined his clothes, put his business in jeopardy, and endangered his own life by driving too fast afterward. Had he found something else wrong with her car, however, he would have repaired that, too. That is what his knowledge of cars is for. Why should a woman learn to change a flat when the opposite sex (half the world's population) is able and willing to do it for her?

Women let men work for them, think for them, and take on their responsibilities—in fact, they exploit them. Yet, since men are strong, intelligent, and imaginative, while women are weak, unimaginative, and stupid, why isn't it men who exploit women?

Could it be that strength, intelligence, and imagination are not prerequisites for power but merely qualifications for slavery? Could it be that the world is not being ruled by experts but by beings who are not fit for anything else—by women? And if this is so, how do

2

women manage it so that their victims do not feel themselves cheated and humiliated, but rather believe themselves to be what they are least of all—masters of the universe? How do women manage to instill in men this sense of pride and superiority that inspires them to ever greater achievements?

Why are women never unmasked?

What Is Man?

A MAN IS A HUMAN BEING who works. By working, he supports himself, his wife, and his wife's children. A woman, on the other hand, is a human being who does not work—or at least only occasionally. Most of her life she supports neither herself nor her children, let alone her husband.

Any qualities in a man that a woman finds useful, she calls *masculine;* all others, of no use to her or to anyone else for that matter, she chooses to call *effeminate*. A man's appearance has to be *masculine* if he wants to have success with women, and that means it will have to be geared to his one and only *raison d'être*—work. His appearance must conform to each and every task put to him, and he must always be able to fulfill it.

Except at night when the majority of men wear striped pajamas with at most two pairs of pockets, men wear a kind of uniform made of durable, stain-resistant material in brown, blue, or gray. These uniforms, or "suits," have up to ten pockets, in which men carry instruments and tools indispensable for their work. Since a woman does not work, her night or day clothes rarely have pockets.

For social events men are permitted to wear black, a color that shows marks and stains, since on those occasions men are less likely to dirty themselves. Moreover, the bright colors worn by women show to advantage against it. The occasional red or green evening jackets worn by men are acceptable, since, by contrast, all the real men present seem so much more masculine.

The rest of a man's appearance is also adapted to his situation. His hair style requires only fifteen minutes at the barber every two or three weeks. Curls, waves, and tints are not encouraged as they might hinder his work. Men often work in the open air or spend a considerable amount of time in it, hence complicated styles would be a nuisance. Furthermore, it is improbable that such styles would make a hit with women since, unlike men, they never judge the opposite sex from an aesthetic point of view. So most men, after one or two attempts at individuality, realize that women are indifferent to their efforts and revert to a standard style, short or long. The same is true of beards. Only oversensitive men—usually ones with intellectual pretensions—who want to appear mentally tough by letting their facial hair grow indiscriminately wear a full beard for any length of time. It will be tolerated by women, however, for a beard is an important indication of a man's character and therefore of the way in which he might be most easily exploited. (His field of work will usually be that of the neurotic intellectual.)

Generally a man uses an electric razor for about three minutes every morning to keep his beard in check. For his skin, soap and water are considered good enough. All that is required is cleanliness and an absence of make-up so that everyone can see what he is like. As for his fingernails, they should be as short as possible for work.

Apart from a wedding ring—worn to show that he is already being used by a particular woman for a particular purpose—a proper man wears no ornaments. His clumsy, functional watch, worn on the wrist, is hardly decorative. Heavy in design, waterproof, shock-resistant, showing the correct date, it cannot possibly be called an ornament. Usually it was given to him by the woman for whom he works.

5

Shirts, underwear, and socks for real men are so standardized that their only difference is one of size. They can be bought in any shop without difficulty or loss of time. Only in ties is there any degree of freedom—and then a man is usually so unused to choosing that he lets his woman buy them for him.

Anyone visiting this earth from another planet would think it each man's goal to look as much like the next as possible. Yet, to fulfill woman's purposes, masculinity and male usefulness vary to a considerable degree: necessarily, because women, who hardly ever work, need men for everything.

There are men who carefully maneuver a large limousine out of the garage at eight o'clock every morning. Others leave an hour earlier, traveling in a middle-class sedan. Still others leave when it is not yet light, wearing overalls and carrying lunch boxes, to catch buses, subways, or trains to factories or building sites. By a trick of fate, it is always the latter, the poorest, who are exploited by the least attractive women. For, unlike women (who have an eye for money), men notice only woman's external appearance. Therefore, the more desirable women in their own class are always being snatched out from under their noses by men who happen to earn more.

No matter what a particular man does or how he spends his day, he has one thing in common with all other men—he spends it in a degrading manner. And he himself does not gain by it. It is not his own livelihood that matters: he would have to struggle far less for that, since luxuries do not mean anything to him anyway. It is the fact that he does it for others that makes him so tremendously proud. He will undoubtedly have a photograph of his wife and children on his desk, and will miss no opportunity to hand it around.

No matter what a man's job may be—bookkeeper, doctor, bus driver, or managing director—every moment of his life will be spent as a cog in a huge and pitiless system—a system designed to exploit him to the utmost, to his dying day.

It may be interesting to add up figures and make them tally—but surely not year in, year out? How exciting it must be to drive a bus through a busy town! But always the same route, at the same time, in the same town, day after day, year after year? What a magnificent feeling of power to know that countless workers move at one's command! But how would one feel if one suddenly realized one was their prisoner and not their master?

We have long ceased to play the games of childhood. As children, we became bored quickly and changed from one game to another. A man is like a child who is condemned to play the same game for the rest of his life. The reason is obvious: as soon as he is discovered to have a gift for one thing, he is made to specialize. Then, because he can earn more money in that field than another, he is forced to do it forever. If he was good at arithmetic in school, if he had a "head for figures," he will be sentenced to a lifetime of figure work as bookkeeper, mathematician, or computer operator, for there lies his maximum work potential. Therefore, he will add up figures, press buttons, and add up more figures, but he will never be able to say, "I'm bored. I want to do something else!" The woman who is exploiting him will never permit him to look for something else. Driven by this woman, he may engage in a desperate struggle against competitors, to improve his position, and perhaps even become head clerk or managing director of a bank. But isn't the price he is paying for his improved salary rather too high?

A man who changes his way of life, or rather his profession (for life and profession are synonymous to him), is considered unreliable. If he does it more than once, he becomes a social outcast and remains alone.

The fear of being rejected by society must be considerable. Why else will a doctor(who as a child liked to observe tadpoles in jam jars) spend his life opening up nauseating growths, examining and pronouncing on human excretions? Why else does he busy himself night and day with people of such repulsiveness that everyone else is driven away? Does a pianist who, as a child, liked to tinkle on the piano really enjoy playing the same Chopin nocturne over and over again all his life? Why else does a politician who as a schoolboy discovered the techniques of manipulating people successfully continue as an adult, mouthing words and phrases as a minor government functionary? Does he actually enjoy contorting his face and playing the fool and listening to the idiotic chatter of other politicians? Surely he must once have dreamed of a different kind of life. Even if he became President of the United States, wouldn't the price be too high?

No, one can hardly assume men do all this for pleasure and without feeling a desire for change. They do it because they have been *manipulated* into doing it: their whole life is nothing but a series of conditioned reflexes, a series of animal acts. A man who is no longer able to perform these acts, whose earning capacity is lessened, is considered a failure. He stands to lose everything—wife, family, home, his whole purpose in life—all the things, in fact, which give him security.

Of course one might say that a man who has lost his capacity for earning money is automatically freed from his burden and should be glad about this happy ending —but freedom is the last thing he wants. He functions, as we shall see, according to the principle of *pleasure in non-freedom*. To be sentenced to life-long freedom is a worse fate than life-long slavery.

To put it another way: man is always searching for someone or something to enslave him, for only as a slave does he feel secure—and, as a rule, his choice falls on a woman. Who or what is this creature who is responsible for his lowly existence and who, moreover, exploits him in such a way that he only feels safe as her slave, *and her slave alone?*

What Is Woman?

A WOMAN, as we have already said, is, in contrast to a man, a human being who does not work. One might leave it at that, for there isn't much more to say about her, were the basic concept of "human being" not so general and inexact in embracing both "man" and "woman."

Life offers the human being two choices: animal existence—a lower order of life—and spiritual existence. In general, a woman will choose the former and opt for physical well-being, a place to breed, and an opportunity to indulge unhindered in her breeding habits.

At birth, men and women have the same intellectual potential; there is no primary difference in intelligence between the sexes. It is also a fact that potential left to stagnate will atrophy. Women do not use their mental capacity: they deliberately let it disintegrate. After a few years of sporadic training, they revert to a state of irreversible mental torpor.

Why do women not make use of their intellectual potential? For the simple reason that they do not need to. It is not essential for their survival. Theoretically it is possible for a beautiful woman to have less intelligence than a chimpanzee and still be considered an acceptable member of society.

By the age of twelve at the latest, most women have decided to become prostitutes. Or, to put it another way, they have planned a future for themselves which consists of choosing a man and letting him do all the work. In return for his support, they are prepared to let him make use of their vagina at certain given moments. The minute a woman has made this decision she ceases to develop her mind. She may, of course, go on to obtain various degrees and diplomas. These increase her market value in the eyes of men, for men believe that a woman who can recite things by heart must also *know and understand* them. But any real possibility of communication between the sexes ceases at this point. Their paths are divided forever.

One of man's worst mistakes, and one he makes over and over again, is to assume that woman is his equal, that is, a human being of equal mental and emotional capacity. A man may observe his wife, listen to her, judge her feelings by her reactions, but in all this he is judging her only by outward symptoms, for he is using his *own* scale of values.

He knows what *he* would say, think, and do if he were in her shoes. When he looks at her depressing ways of doing things, he assumes there must be something that prevents her from doing what he himself would have done in her position. This is natural, as he considers himself the measure of all things—and rightly so—if humans define themselves as beings capable of abstract thought.

When a man sees a woman spending hours cooking, washing dishes, and cleaning, it never occurs to him that such jobs probably make her quite happy since they are exactly at her mental level. Instead he assumes that this drudgery prevents her from doing all those things which he himself considers worthwhile and desirable. Therefore, he invents automatic dishwashers, vacuum cleaners, and precooked foods to make her life easier and to allow her to lead the dream life he himself longs for.

But he will be disappointed: rarely using the time she has gained to take an active interest in history, politics, or astrophysics, woman bakes cakes, irons underclothes, and makes ruffles and frills for blouses or, if she is especially enterprising, covers her bathroom with flower decals. It is natural, therefore, that man assumes such things to be the essential ingredients of *gracious living*. This idea must have been instilled by woman, as he himself really doesn't mind if his cakes are store-bought, his underpants unironed, or his bathroom devoid of flowery patterns. He invents cake mixes to liberate her from drudgery, automatic irons and toilet-paper holders already covered with flower patterns to make gracious living easier to attain—and still women take no interest in serious literature, politics, or the conquest of the universe. For her, this newfound leisure comes at just the right moment. At last she can take an interest in *herself:* since a longing after intellectual achievements is alien to her, she concentrates on her external appearance.

Yet even this occupation is acceptable to man. He really loves his wife and wants her happiness more than anything in the world. Therefore, he produces non-smear lipstick, waterproof mascara, home permanents, no-iron frilly blouses, and throwaway underwear—always with the same aim in view. In the end, he hopes, this being whose needs seem to him so much more sensitive, so much more refined, will gain freedom—freedom to achieve in *her* life the ideal state which is *his* dream: to live the life of a *free* man.

Then he sits back and waits. Finally, as woman does not come to him of her own free will, he tries to tempt her into his world. He offers her coeducation, so that she is accustomed to his way of life from childhood. With all sorts of excuses, he gets her to attend his universities and initiates her into the mysteries of his own discoveries, hoping to awaken her interest in the wonders of life. He gives her access to the very last male strongholds, thereby relinquishing traditions sacred to him by encouraging her to make use of her right to vote in the hope that she will change the systems of government he has managed to think up so laboriously, according to her own ideas. Possibly he even hopes that she will be able to create peace in the world—for, in his opinion, women are a pacifist influence.

In all this he is so determined and pigheaded that he fails to see what a fool he is making of himself—ridiculous by his own standards, not those of women, who have absolutely no sense of humor.

No, women do not laugh at men. At most they get irritated. The old institutions of house and home are not yet so obviously outdated and derelict that they can't justify relinquishing all their intellectual pursuits and renouncing all their claims to better jobs. One does wonder, however, what will happen when housework is still further mechanized, when there are *enough* good nursery schools nearby, or when—as must occur before long—men discover that children themselves are not essential.

If only man would stop for one moment in his heedless rush toward progress and think about this state of affairs, he would inevitably realize that his efforts to give woman a sense of mental stimulation have been totally in vain. It is true that woman gets progressively more elegant, more well-groomed, more "cultured," but her demands on life will always be material, never intellectual.

Has she ever made use of the mental processes he teaches at his universities to develop her own theories? Does she do independent research in the institutes he has thrown open to her? Someday it will dawn on man that woman does not read the wonderful books with which he has filled his libraries. And though she may well admire his marvelous works of art in museums, she herself will rarely create, only copy. Even the plays and films, visual exhortations to woman on her own level to liberate herself, are judged only by their entertainment value. They will never be a first step to revolution.

When a man, believing woman his equal, realizes

the futility of her way of life, he naturally tends to think that it must be *his* fault, that *he* must be suppressing *her*. But in our time women are no longer subject to the will of men. Quite the contrary. They have been given every opportunity to win their independence and if, after all this time, they have not liberated themselves and thrown off their shackles, we can only arrive at one conclusion: there are no shackles to throw off.

It is true that men love women, but they also despise them. Anyone who gets up in the morning fresh and ready to conquer new worlds (with infrequent success, admittedly, because he has to earn a living) is bound to despise someone who simply isn't interested in such pursuits. Contempt may even be one of the main reasons for his efforts to further the mental development of a woman. He feels ashamed of her and assumes that she, too, must be ashamed of herself. So, being a gentleman, he tries to help.

Men seem incapable of realizing that women entirely lack ambition, desire for knowledge, and need to prove themselves, all things which, to him, are a matter of course. They allow men to live in a world apart because they do not want to join them. Why should they? The sort of independence men have means nothing to women, because women don't feel dependent. They are not even embarrassed by the intellectual superiority of men because they have no ambition in that direction.

There is one great advantage which women have over men: *they have a choice*—a choice between the life of a man and the life of a dimwitted, parasitic luxury item. There are too few women who would not select the latter. Men do not have this choice.

If women really felt oppressed by men, they would have developed hate and fear for them, as the oppressed always do, but women do not fear men, much less hate them. If they really felt humiliated by men's mental superiority, they would have used every means in their power to change the situation. If women really felt unfree, surely, at such a favorable time in their history, they would have broken free of their oppressors.

In Switzerland, one of the most highly developed countries of the world, where until recently women were not allowed to vote, in a certain canton, it is reported, the majority of women were against introducing the vote for women. The Swiss men were shattered, for they saw in this unworthy attitude yet another proof of centuries of male oppression.

How very wrong they were! Women feel anything but oppressed by men. On the contrary, one of the many depressing truths about the relationship between the sexes is simply that man hardly exists in a woman's world: Man is not even powerful enough to revolt against. Woman's dependence on him is only material, of a "physical" nature, something like a tourist's dependence on an airline, a café proprietor's on his espresso machine, a car's on gasoline, a television set's on electric current. Such dependencies hardly involve agonizing.

Ibsen, who suffered from the same misapprehensions as other men, meant his *Doll's House* to be a kind of manifesto for the freedom of women. The première in 1880 certainly shocked *men,* and they determined to fight harder to improve women's position.

For women themselves, however, the struggle for emancipation as usual took shape in a change of style: for a while they delighted in their often-laughed-at masquerade as suffragettes.

Later on, the philosophy of Sartre made a similarly profound impression on women. As proof that they understood it completely, they let their hair grow down to their waists and wore black pullovers and trousers.

Even the teachings of the Chinese Communist leader Mao Tse-tung were a success—the Mao look lasted for a whole season.

The Horizon of a Woman

WHATEVER MEN SET ABOUT to impress women with counts for nothing in the world of women. Only another woman is of importance in her world.

Of course, a woman will always be pleased if a man turns to look at her—and if he is well dressed or drives an expensive sports car, so much the better. Her pleasure may be compared to that of a shareholder who finds that his stocks have risen. It will be a matter of complete indifference to a woman if he is attractive or looks intelligent. A shareholder is hardly likely to notice the color of his dividend checks.

But if another woman should turn to look—a rare occurrence, for her own judgment is infinitely more remorseless than that of a man—her day is made. She has achieved the impossible—the recognition, admiration, and "love" of other women.

Yes, only women exist in a woman's world. The women she meets at church, at parent-teacher meetings, or in the supermarket; the women with whom she chats over the garden fence; the women at parties or window-shopping in the more fashionable streets; those she apparently never seems to notice—these women are the measure of her success or failure. Women's standards correspond to those in other women's heads, not to those in the heads of men; it is *their* judgment that really counts, not that of men. A simple word of praise from another woman—and all those clumsy, inadequate male compliments fall by the wayside, for they are just praises out of the mouths of amateurs. Men really have no idea of what a woman's world means; their fulsome compliments miss all the vital points.

Of course woman wants to please man as well: don't let us forget, after all, that he provides the material means. But that is much more easily done. Men have been conditioned to react to a certain degree of differentiation: they expect women to conform to certain types of sex symbols created by make-up and other standard trappings: long hair, painted lips, tight-fitting sweaters, miniskirts, sheer stockings, high heels—all done in a moment.

It is those living works of art which are beyond man's comprehension—those creatures walking the fashionable streets of Paris, Rome, and New York. The skill of eyeliner and shadow expertly applied; the choice of lipstick and its application, with or without lipbrush, in several layers or only in one; the compromise to be achieved between the pros and cons of false eyelashes, the matching of a dress, a stole, or a coat with the lighting—all this is an art requiring expert knowledge of which man has no conception. A man lacks any kind of appreciation for this. He has not learned to interpret the extent of female masquerades, and he cannot possibly evaluate these walking works of art. To achieve perfection such skill needs time, money, and an infinitely limited mind—and these requirements are met only by women.

In fact, when a woman dresses, she considers a man only to a slight extent—the extent necessary to hold him and to encourage him to provide (in the widest sense) for her. Every other investment is aimed at other women. Man has importance only as the provider.

If a firm wants to get hold of a specialist in some field, it will flatter and entice him in every possible way until he weakens. Once the contract is signed, his employers can relax. Their leverage over him continues to increase. A woman behaves in much the same way with a man. She gives her man just enough rope to ensure his preferring life by her side to breaking his contract with her.

A woman may, in fact, be compared to a firm in a number of ways. After all, a firm is only an impersonal system aimed at achieving a maximum profit. And what else does a woman do? Without any emotion—love, hate, or malice—she is bound to the man who works for her. Feelings become involved only if he threatens to leave her. Then her livelihood is at stake. As this is a rational reaction with a rational cause, it can be rationally dealt with and adjusted to. She can always place another man under contract. How different is her reaction from those of a man who finds himself in a similar position. He is racked by jealousy, humiliation, feelings of inferiority and self-pity—but she as emotionless.

A woman would hardly ever feel jealous in such a situation, since the man is leaving her only for another woman and not in order to be free. In her eyes he is not improving his position in any way. The adventure of a man's love for a new woman is nothing more than a nuisance. She is seeing it all from the angle of the small entrepreneur who loses his best worker to a competitor. As far as a woman is concerned, the heartache involved is nothing more than a reaction to letting good business go elsewhere.

Consequently, it is quite absurd for any man to think his wife is being *faithful* merely because she does not go off with other men—men who, in his eyes, are more attractive. Provided he is working hard and is supplying all the things that really matter to her, why should she? A woman's faithfulness has nothing in common with that of a man. Women are, in contrast to men, practically immune to the looks of the opposite sex. If a woman flirts with her husband's best friend, her intention is to annoy his wife, whose feelings do matter, unlike those of her own husband. If she felt deeply

17

about the man in question, she would never show her emotions in public.

In pluralistic sex practices such as wife-swapping, which has now taken over from flirtation as a pastime, it is the other wife who is the object of attack. History is full of anecdotes about male potentates enjoying themselves with many mistresses at the same time, but there are few such stories about female potentates. A woman would be bored to tears with an all-male harem. This has always been the case and will remain so.

If women reacted to a man's *external* appearance, every current advertisement scheme would be useless. According to statistics, it is the female sector of the population who spends the most money—money men earn for them. Manufacturers do not attempt to stimulate sales by advertisements displaying handsome he-men. On the contrary. No matter what they want to sell—tours, detergents, cars, bedroom suites, television sets—each advertisement flaunts a beautiful woman.

Only very recently have film producers realized that a handsome hero is not essential to the success of a film. Women are quite content with an ugly star— Jean-Paul Belmondo, Walter Matthau, or Dustin Hoffman. And naturally men prefer them. With their sense of physical inferiority due to the fact that they only very rarely consider themselves beautiful, they find it far easier to identify with a homely star. As long as there is a beautiful female lead, a film with a homely male star will be enjoyed by women as much as a movie starring Rock Hudson. For, in reality, they are interested only in the women in the film.

The reason men have remained blind to facts like these for such a long time is that they have been misled by the attacks women make on each other. When they hear a woman make derogatory remarks about another—her nose is too big, chest too flat, hips too wide, legs crooked—men, of course, assume that they can't stand each other or that women are not attracted by another woman's beauty.

Yet how wrong they are. Any businessman, for example, who spends his life praising his competitors in front of his employees would be thought quite mad. Before long, half his best workers would have moved to the other firm. It is the same game that politicians play. Of course they have to blacken each other's names, but if Nixon got stranded on a desert island, he would surely prefer the company of Kosygin or Castro to the much praised man-in-the-street who only elected him. After all, they have very little in common.

If women were free of financial cares, probably the majority of them would prefer to spend their lives in the company of other women rather than with men— and not because they are all lesbians. What men call lesbian tendencies probably have little to do with a woman's sexual drive. No—the sexes have almost no interests in common. What, besides money, can bind a woman to a man?

Women make ideal living companions for each other. Their feelings and instincts are retarded at the same primitive level, and there are almost no individualistic or eccentric women. It isn't difficult to imagine the paradise they would create together and how exciting their existence would be, even if the intellectual level was appallingly low. Who would worry about it?

The Fair Sex

To someone from outer space surely men would appear infinitely more worthy of admiration than women, for man has intelligence as well as beauty. Throughout the centuries man's standard of values must have become sadly confused, otherwise women would never have been called the fair sex. The mere fact that they are so much less intelligent than men is enough to contradict such a conception, for a stupid person can never be thought of as beautiful unless judged on the purely physical level. But it should be emphasized that the fault lies with man himself, who valued women according to standards by which people and animals are on the same level. If he had not done so, women would hardly fit into the group Homo sapiens.

A man needs a woman because, as we shall see, he needs something to which he may subject himself. But at the same time he must retain his self-respect. This leads him to endow woman with qualities which will justify his subjection. As woman has never yet made any attempt to use her wits, he cannot call her intelligent, but he gets close to it by creating the concept of "woman's intuition." So, in the absence of any other real qualities, he calls her beautiful.

Aesthetic standards are necessarily subjective and each aesthetic judgment one makes is an act of personal choice. But subjectivity easily turns into an excuse, and man is only too pleased to allow himself to become a slave. A man assumes that, since woman adorns herself with the obvious intention of drawing all eyes toward her, she must have some reason for her action. So man finds woman beautiful because she thinks she is beautiful. Indeed, he is very grateful for being allowed to share this opinion.

But this feminine claim to beauty is also supported by subterfuge, by a trick. Woman's greatest ideal is a life without work or responsibility—yet who leads such a life but a child? A child with appealing eyes, a funny little body with dimples and sweet layers of baby fat and clear, taut skin—that darling miniature of an adult. It is a child that woman imitates—its easy laugh, its helplessness, its need for protection. A child must be cared for; it cannot look after itself. And what species does not, by natural instinct, look after its offspring? It must—or the species will die out.

With the aid of skillfully applied cosmetics, designed to preserve that precious baby look; with the aid of helpless, appealing babble and exclamations such as "Ooh" and "Ah," to denote astonishment, surprise, and admiration; with inane little bursts of conversation, women have preserved this "baby look" for as long as possible so as to make the world continue to believe in the darling, sweet little girl she once was, and she relies on the protective instinct in man to make him take care of her.

As with everything a woman undertakes on her own initiative, this whole maneuver is as incredible as it is stupid. It is amazing, in fact, that it succeeds. It would also appear very shortsighted to encourage such an ideal of beauty. For how can any woman hope to maintain it beyond the age of twenty-five? Despite every trick of the cosmetics industry, despite magazine advice against thinking or laughing (both tend to create wrinkles), her actual age will inevitably show through in the end. And what on earth is a man to do with a grownup face when he has been manipulated into considering only helpless, appealing little girls to be creatures of beauty?

What is a man to do with a woman when the smooth curves have become flabby tires of flesh, the skin slack and pallid, when the childish tones have grown shrill, and the laughter sounds like neighing? What is to become of this shrew when her face no longer atones for her ceaseless inanities and when the cries of "Ooh" and "Ah" begin to drive him out of his mind? This mummified "child" will never fire a man's erotic fantasy again. One might think her power broken at last.

But no, she still manages to get her own way—and for two reasons. The first is obvious: she now has children, who enable her to continue feigning helplessness. As for the second—there are simply not enough *young* women to go around.

It's a safe bet that, given the choice, man would trade in his grownup child-wife for a younger model, but, as the ratio between the sexes is roughly equal, not every man can have a younger woman. And as he has to have a wife of some sort, he prefers to keep the one he already possesses.

This is easy to prove. Given the choice, a man will always choose a younger woman. Elizabeth Taylor and Marilyn Monroe were passé the moment their wrinkles could no longer be hidden by layers of make-up and, therefore, when a man went to the cinema, he simply bought a ticket to see a younger star. Anyone who can afford it is not restricted in this respect to buying seats at cinemas. Financiers and show-business tycoons make a habit of turning in their used wives for newer models, and, since alimony is fairly good, not even the old wife seems to mind; in fact she is probably very glad to have made such a good bargain.

But this is a luxury for the rich alone. If a poor man decides, in a moment of euphoric irresponsibility, to change over to a younger woman, he can be sure of losing her pretty quickly. His money will never stretch to two wives and two sets of children, for the second

wife will certainly insist on having offspring as well.
And if an attractive young woman has a choice, she
will choose a young man every time, providing he is financially secure. This is not, of course, for aesthetic
reasons. With any luck, he will be able to provide for
her longer. On the other hand, if offered a rich man of
forty, a woman will certainly prefer him to a poor
young man of twenty. Women certainly know what
they want from men and know exactly on which side
their bread is buttered.

It is lucky for the adult woman that men do not consider themselves beautiful, since most men are beautiful. Their smooth bodies, kept trim by hard work, their
strong shoulders, their muscular legs, their melodic
voices, their warm, human laughter, the intelligent ex-
pression of their faces, and their calibrated, meaningful
movements overshadow those of women completely,
even in a purely animal sense. And since they, unlike
women, work and their bodies are therefore preserved
for continued future use, men also retain their beauty
longer. As a result of their inertia, women's bodies rapidly decay and, after the age of fifty, they are nothing
but indifferent heaps of human cells. (One has only to
observe a fifty-year-old housewife on the street and
compare her appearance with that of a man of the
same age.)

Men are not aware of their own beauty and no one
mentions it. There is so much rubbish written and
talked about the charm of women. Even children and
animals are considered graceful, adorable, and delight-
ful—but never a man. Men are at best praised for their
steadfastness, courage, reliability—all qualities useful to
women, having nothing to do with physical appearance.
It would be difficult to find a description of the male
body except in a medical textbook. And outside of
these, who would ever dream of going into great detail
about the exact shape of his lips, the precise shade of his
eyes in a special kind of light? And as for the delicacy of

23

his nipples or the pleasing shape of his scrotum and his testicles—just imagine a man's amazement and amusement if they were the subject of hymns of praise!

Men are not used to having their looks discussed. Grown women, as a rule ugly creatures, have time and opportunity to admire men, but rarely see them. It is not that a woman is mean or envious; it is that she thinks of him as a machine—a machine for the production of material goods. And who regards a machine as an object of beauty? It is something that functions, and men judge themselves similarly. They are far too worn out by their role as providers and by the eternal rat race to think of being objective about their own looks.

All this is a pointless discussion anyway, for basically men are not interested in the possibility of being beautiful. What point would that give to their labors? Women *must* be the ones who are beautiful, helpless, adorable—they must be, in fact, lacking a more precise definition, "the fair sex."

It's a Man's Universe

MAN, UNLIKE WOMAN, is beautiful, because man, unlike woman, is a thinking creature.

This means:

Man has a thirst for knowledge (he wants to know what the world around him looks like and how it functions).

Man thinks (he draws conclusions from the data he encounters).

Man is creative (he makes something new out of the information achieved by the above processes).

Man is sensitive (as a result of his exceptionally wide, multidimensional emotional scale, he not only registers the commonplace in fine gradations but he creates and discovers new emotional values and makes them accessible to others through sensible descriptions, or re-creates them as an artist.

Of all the qualities of man, his curiosity is certainly the most impressive. This curiosity differs basically from that of woman.

A woman takes interest only in subjects that have an immediate personal usefulness to her. For example, if she reads a political article in the newspaper, it is highly likely that she wants to cast a spell on some political-science student, not that she cares about the fate of the Chinese, Israelis, or South Africans. If she looks up the names of some Greek philosophers in the dictionary, it does not mean she has suddenly taken an interest in Greek philosophy. It means she is trying to solve a crossword puzzle. If she is studying the ads for a new car, she is not doing it with a platonic interest in its technical features, but because she wants to own it.

It is a fact that most women—mothers included—generally have no idea how the human fetus is formed, how it develops in the womb, what stages it passes through before birth. Of course it is entirely unnecessary for her to know about these things, since they cannot influence the development of the embryo anyway. It is only important to know that a pregnancy lasts nine months and that for the duration one must take care of oneself and, in case of complications, immediately consult one's doctor, who will, of course, restore everything to order.

Man's curiosity is something quite different. His desire for knowledge has no personal implications, is purely objective, and, in the long run, is much more practical than a woman's attitude.

One has only to watch a man go past a building site where a newly developed machine is being used, for example a new kind of dredger. There is hardly a man—regardless of social status—who will pass by without a glance. Many will stop to have a good look and to discuss the characteristics of the new machine, its advantages and disadvantages, and its differences from previous models.

A woman would never think of stopping at a building site unless, of course, the crowd was so big that she thought she might miss something exciting ("Construction Worker Crushed by Bulldozer"). In that case she would demand to know all the details and then look the other way.

Man's curiosity is universal. There is almost nothing that does not interest him, whether it is politics, botany, nuclear physics, or God knows what. Even subjects out

26

of his province hold his interest, such as bottling fruit, preparing a cake mix, or caring for a baby. And a man could not be pregnant for nine months without knowing all the functions of the placenta and ovaries.

Men not only observe the world around them, it is in their nature to make comparisons and to apply the knowledge they have gained elsewhere with the ultimate aim to transform this newfound knowledge into something else, something new.

One need not emphasize the fact that practically all the inventions and discoveries in this world have been made by men, and not only in the fields of electricity, aerodynamics, gynecology, cybernetics, mathematics, quantum mechanics, hydraulics, and the origin of the species. In addition, men have devised the principles of child psychology and infant nutrition, as well as pasteurization and other means of preserving food. Even the changes in women's fashions or other such trivial matters as the creation of new menus and palatal nuances are traditionally the province of men. If one wishes to have an unusual culinary treat, generally one will not find it at home but at a restaurant, where, of course, the chef is male. A woman's sense of taste is so blunted and deadened by the repetitive preparation of unimaginative, run-of-the-mill, tasteless, everyday cooking that, even if she wanted to try out new foods, she would not be capable of it. There is no female gourmet; women are good for almost nothing.

With his many gifts man would appear to be ideally suited, both mentally and physically, to lead a life both fulfilled and free. Instead he chooses to become a slave, placing his many discoveries at the service of those who are incapable of creation themselves—at the service of "mankind," man's own synonym for women, and of the children of these women.

How paradoxical that this very sex, which is capable of leading a life as nearly perfect as possible, is prepared to give it up, to offer it all to the female sex, which is not interested in such perfection. We have grown so accustomed to the blunted mechanism of onesided exploitation of one group of human beings by a parasitic clique that all our moral values have become completely perverted.

Without really giving the matter any thought, we consider the male sex as a kind of Sisyphus: he has come into the world to learn, to work, and to father children: his sons, in their turn, will learn to work and produce children, and so it will continue forever; it has become almost impossible to think why else men should be here.

If a young man gets married, starts a family, and spends the rest of his life working at a soul-destroying job, he is held up as an example of virtue and responsibility. The other type of man, living only for himself, working only for himself, doing first one thing and then another simply because he enjoys it and because he has to keep only himself, sleeping where and when he wants, and facing woman when he meets her, on equal terms and not as one of a million slaves, is rejected by society. The free, unshackled man has no place in its midst.

How depressing it is to see men, year after year, betraying all that they were born to. New worlds could be discovered, worlds one hardly dares even to dream of could be opened by the minds, strength, and intelligence of men. Things to make life fuller and richer— their own life, that is, of which women are ignorant— and more worthwhile could be developed: all these things could be done by men. Instead, they forsake all these tremendous potentials and permit their minds and their bodies to be shunted onto sidings to serve the repulsively primitive needs of women. Man has the key to every mystery of the universe in his hand, but he ignores it, he lowers himself to the level of woman and insinuates himself into her favor.

With his mind, his strength, and his imagination, all intended for the creation of *new* worlds, he opts instead for the preservation and improvement of the *old*. And

if he happens to invent something new, he needs to pre-
fix it with the excuse that it will one day be useful to
"all mankind," i.e., to women. He apologizes for his
achievements, for making space flights instead of
providing more comforts for his wife and children. The
most tiresome aspect of technological advances is having to translate them for television ads into female language composed of children's prattle and sweet
lovetalk. Man is begging woman to be patient with him
and his discoveries, or at least to buy them. Women's
proven lack of imagination makes clear that they have
no *a priori* need for new inventions. If they did, they
would invent things more often themselves.

We are so accustomed to men doing everything with
women in view that anything else seems unthinkable.
For example, couldn't composers create something
apart from *love* (dependency) songs? Couldn't writers
give up their romantic novels and *love* (dependency)
poems and try to write literature? Can painters only
produce nudes and profiles of women, abstract or real-
istic? Why can't we have something *new* after all this
time, something we have never seen before?

It should really be possible for scientists to forget
dedicating their works to their wives; anyhow, they will
never, never be able to understand them. When will the
time come when experimental films have no longer to
be weighted down by sexy female bodies, when news
reports on space travel do not need to be encumbered
with interviews of peroxided astronauts' wives? Even
the astronauts themselves might stop having schmaltzy
love (dependency) songs played to them during their
interplanetary travels.

We have absolutely no idea what the world would be
like if men really used their intelligence and imagination instead of wasting it. Inventing pressure cookers
that cook faster, wall-to-wall carpeting that is more
stain-resistant, detergents that wash whiter, and lipsticks that are more water-resistant *is* a waste of time.
Instead of producing children who will in turn produce

29

children, thus pushing the enjoyment of life still further out of their own reach, they should try living *themselves*. Instead of probing the depth of woman's "mysterious" psyche—"mysterious" only because there is nothing behind it—they should study their own psyche, perhaps even that of creatures possibly inhabiting other planets, and think out new ways and means of establishing contact with *them*. Instead of inventing ever more deadly weapons to fight wars destined only to defend private property, i.e., women's, they should be developing ever more efficient methods of space travel—travel which would tell us more about worlds we never dreamed of.

Unfortunately, men who are capable and willing to work and think in every other field of research have declared everything concerning woman taboo. What is worse is that this taboo has always been so effective that it is no longer recognized as such. *Women's* wars, *women's* children, *women's* towns—all these are made by men. Women just sit back getting lazier, dumber, and more demanding—and, at the same time, richer. A primitive but effective system of insurance policies—policies for marriage, divorce, inheritance, widowhood, old age, and life—ensures this increasing wealth. For example, in the U.S.A. half of the total private capital is in the hands of women. Yet the number of working women has constantly decreased over the last decades. The situation is not much different in industrial Europe. At this time women already have complete psychological control over men. It won't be long before they have material control as well.

Men seem to be quite unaware of these facts and go on finding happiness in their own subjugation. There could be justification for their attitude only if women really were the charming, gracious creatures men believe them to be: fairy princesses, angels from another world, too good both for men themselves and for this earthly existence.

It is quite incredible that men, whose desire for

knowledge is unbounded in every other field, are really totally blind to these facts, that they are incapable of seeing women as they really are: with nothing else to offer but a vagina, two breasts, and some punch cards programmed with idle, stereotyped chatter; that they are nothing more than conglomerations of matter, lumps of stuffed human skin pretending to be thinking human beings.

If men would only stop for a moment in their head-long creativity and think, they could easily tear the masks off these creatures with their tinkling bracelets, frilly blouses, and gold-leather sandals. Surely it would take them only a couple of days, considering their own intelligence, imagination, and determination, to construct a machine, a kind of human female robot to take the place of woman. For there is nothing original in her—neither inside nor out—which could not be replaced. Why are men so afraid to face the truth?

Ira Levin's
The Stepford Wives

Woman—
Divine by Right of Stupidity

ONLY THE OPPRESSED have any real need of freedom. Yet as soon as they are free—and providing they have the intelligence to weigh their freedom against the possible consequences—this need changes. The former longing for freedom reverts to a sense of fear accompanied by an intense longing to be tied and secure.

In the first years of life man is never free. He is hemmed in by adult rules and, having no experience of social conduct to guide him, he is entirely dependent on them. As a result he develops an acute desire for freedom and feels a desperate need to escape from his prison at the first opportunity.

Once a human being is free, if it happens to be rather stupid (and women *are stupid*) it will be quite happy with its freedom and try to retain it. As the unintelligent human being is incapable of abstract thought, it will never feel the need to leave its familiar terrain and consequently will never fear that its very existence might be threatened. It is not afraid of death because it cannot imagine it. There is no need to find a meaning or reason for life: its desires are fulfilled in its own personal comforts, and these provide reason enough for living. Even the need for religion is comparatively unknown to a person of low intelligence and, if it does arise, it is very easily satisfied. A stupid person has an infinite capacity for self-adoration. If a woman chooses to believe in God, it is for one reason only: she wants to go to heaven. And what, after all, is the dear Lord but yet another man who will arrange things for her?

The situation of the intelligent person, i.e., a man, is very different. At first he welcomes his newfound freedom with a sense of relief, drunk with the vision and perspective of life before him. But the moment he puts this freedom to the test, that is, as soon as he wants to commit a given act which might send him in a given direction, he gets scared: since he is capable of abstract thought, he knows that each of his acts has a series of possible consequences, not all of which can be predicted. If he decides to act of his own free will, the responsibility will be his alone.

At that moment, man would be delighted to cease all activity, but, because he is a man and it is man's destiny to act, he begins to long for the rules of his childhood, to long for someone who will tell him what to do, to give meaning to his now meaningless actions. These actions are meaningless because they serve his comfort, but what does he serve? At this point he will search for a new deity, one to take the place of his mother, the deity of his childhood. The moment he finds her, he becomes her abject slave.

Given the choice, of course, man would prefer a deity that is strong, just, wise, and omniscient—rather like the God of Christians, Jews, and Mohammedans. But as he is an intelligent being, he knows that such a deity cannot exist, that every adult is, by definition, his own personal deity who must make his own rules. Every adult, i.e., every man, must satisfy his *craving for non-freedom*, a regression to a sort of infantile dependency which gives him pleasure, and he can do this only by imposing rules (deities) on himself, which he then sets out to fabricate.

When man creates rules he unconsciously compares experiences with other men. Finding something in common with them, he derives generalizations. These "rules" become laws for future "reasonable" conduct (in other words, beneficial to someone other than himself), to which he voluntarily subjects himself. The systems thus created grow collectively and individually more broadly applicable, and soon they are so complex that the individual details are no longer distinguishable: they achieve autonomy and become "divine." One can only *believe* in these laws—just as an inexperienced child must *believe* in the partly senseless, partly sensible rules of its parents. To trespass carries the threat of exclusion from society and loss of security. Marxism, brotherly love, racism, and nationalism all evolved in this way. A man whose personal need for religion is satisfied by such larger systems will be relatively safe from subjection to the rule of an individual (woman).

The majority of men prefer to subjugate themselves to an exclusive deity, *woman* (they call this subjection *love*). This sort of personal deity has excellent qualifications for the satisfaction of religious needs. Woman is ever-present, and, given her own lack of religious need, she is divine. As she continuously makes demands, man never feels forsaken. She frees him from collective gods, for whose favors he would have to compete with others. He trusts in her because she resembles his mother, the deity of his childhood. His empty life is given an artificial meaning, for his every action is dedicated to *her* comfort and, later, to the comfort of her children. As a goddess, she can not only punish (by taking away his sense of belonging) but she can reward as well (through the bestowal of sexual pleasure).

The most important requirements for woman's divinity are, however, her propensity to masquerade and her stupidity. A system must either overwhelm its believers with its greatly superior wisdom or confuse them with its incomprehensibility. As the first possibility is unavailable to women, they take advantage of the second. Their masquerade causes them to appear strange and mysterious to men; their stupidity makes them inaccessible to scrutiny. While intelligence shows itself in actions that are reasonable and logical, hence permits measurement, predictability, and control, stupidity shows itself in actions that are completely unreasonable, unpredictable, and uncontrollable. Women are protected by a screen of pomp, mummery, and mystification as much as any Pope or dictator: they cannot be unmasked and will increase their power unhindered, gaining strength as they go. In return man is guaranteed, for the duration, a divinity in which he can deeply believe.

Breaking Them In

To ENSURE that the happiness of man in subjugation is brought about by a woman and not by other men or some sort of animal, or even by one of the above-mentioned social systems, into man's life are built a series of training exercises, whose practice begins at a very early age. It is fortunate for woman that the male infant is under her close jurisdiction as it is easiest to train him then. And by the natural process of selection, the very women who are best suited to training men are the ones who reproduce themselves; the others are incapable of reproducing themselves.

The mere fact that a man is accustomed from his earliest years to have women around, to find their presence "normal," their absence "abnormal," tends to make him dependent on women in later life. But this dependency would not be serious, for a life without women would in that case mean nothing more than a change of scenery, just as someone born in the mountains might go and live in the plains: although he might long nostalgically for his mountain home, he is unlikely to go back. Other things become more important in his life.

It would hardly be in the best interests of women if they only inspired in men a vague romantic nostalgia, felt only on Sundays or when away from home, having no direct consequences. She takes care that man is directly trained for a particular purpose: he must work and put the fruits of his labor at her disposal. Woman has had this aim in view throughout the upbringing of her child, and she engenders in him a series of conditioned reflexes which cause him to produce everything to satisfy her material needs. She does this by manipulating him from his first year of life. Consequently, by the time his education is complete, man will judge his own value by woman's estimation of his usefulness. He will be happy only when he has won her praise and produced something of value to her.

One might well say that woman becomes a kind of value scale. At a given moment, a man can refer back to it and judge the value or futility of his actions. If he spends any time on something which has no value in terms of this chart, football, for example, he will do his best to compensate quickly for this minus point by increasing his activity on the plus side of the scale—which explains why women do not object too strongly to football or other types of spectator sports.

One of the most useful factors in the conditioning of a man is *praise*. Its effect is better and much more lasting than say, sex, as it may be continued throughout a man's life. Furthermore, if praise is applied in the correct dosage, a woman will never need to scold. Any man who is accustomed to a conditional dosage of praise will interpret its absence as displeasure.

Training by means of praise has the following advantages: it makes the object of praise dependent (for praise to be worth something, it has to come from a higher source, thus the object of praise lifts the praise-giver to a superior level); it creates an addict (without praise, he soon no longer knows whether or not he is worth something and forgets the ability to identify with himself); it increases his productivity (praise is most effectively meted out not for the same achievements, but for increasingly higher ones).

The moment a male child has been rewarded by a warm smile and by the customary inane kind of encouraging adult baby talk for using his pot and not

37

wetting his bed, or for drinking the last drop in his bottle, he is caught up in a vicious circle. He will repeat the actions which called forth praise and endearments and, if at any time recognition is not granted, he will do everything in his power to regain it. The happiness he feels when praise is restored will already have assumed the proportions of an addiction.

During the first two years of life, a mother does not discriminate between boys and girls. The female infant is submitted to the same form of manipulation until the principles of hygiene are absorbed, but from that moment on, the education of the two sexes follows very different paths. The older the girl grows, the more highly conditioned she becomes in the art of exploiting others, while a boy is increasingly manipulated into becoming an object of exploitation.

Toys play an important part in this early manipulation. The mother will first stimulate the playfulness of her children, and then she will exploit it. The girl child will be given dolls with all the necessary paraphernalia—prams, dolls' beds, and miniature tea-sets. The boy will be given everything a girl never has—Meccano sets, electric trains, miniature race cars, and airplanes. Thus the girl is conditioned right from the start to identify with her mother, to fit herself into the role of woman. Dolls are praised or scolded as Mother praises and scolds. It's child's play to her to absorb the principles of leadership; a girl's education, like a boy's, is based on praise, meted out to her, however, only when she identifies with the female role, so that she will never want to be anything but "feminine." The standard set of values will inevitably be woman's forever, since only women can judge how good their own role is (men are taught that woman's role is inferior; hence there is no cause to praise women).

A male child is constantly praised for everything, except for playing with miniature humans. He builds model dams, bridges, and canals, takes toy cars apart to see how they work, shoots toy pistols, and practices

Manipulation
by Means of Self-Abasement

A CRITICAL MAN might well say that women have no self-respect. If they had, they would never admit the incredible extent of their ignorance as happily as they do. How easily man forgets that his own standards of honor, pride, and dignity are all instilled in him by women and that the very masculinity of which he is so proud is but a sign of successful manipulation! No credit goes to him at all.

Any psychology textbook will tell us that a child's ability to achieve something is best enhanced by giving that child self-confidence. This, however, is not something he can acquire by himself. He is born into a society on which he is dependent for everything, a society in which his own powers are insufficient to get what he wants unaided. So, as a woman's first interest lies in creating an adult capable not only of providing for himself, but for others as well, it is of utmost importance to instill self-confidence in this youth. She starts by minimizing the dangers of life—insofar as she herself is aware of them. She closes his eyes to the possibility of death, or promises him eternal life as a reward for being good—good, that is, by her standards. She tries as hard as she can to give him a sense of imbecile optimism that will best prepare him for her manipulation—and for life in general.

As we have already seen, praise is one of the best

ways of inducing self-confidence—and of enhancing productivity. There is another method which is as effective: self-abasement on the part of a woman.

If a woman were not superior to her child, at least in the early stages of his development, the human race would cease to exist. A good mother will take the greatest care, however, never to let this fact impede her child's development. She does not want to turn the tables on herself and keep the boy tied to her apron strings for longer than necessary. As soon as possible she will try to give a male child a sense of superiority toward herself—a kind of advance against achievements to come. This gives him his first experience of confidence. She may even go one step further and deliberately pretend to be less intelligent than she is, giving him a head start he will never lose. This, of course, is providing he grows up to be a proper man—and she will take care of that.

As the value of woman in society is not measured by intelligence but by completely different standards (in fact, there are no standards: man needs her, and that is enough), she may be as stupid, in appearance or in reality, as suits her convenience. This is something women have in common with the wealthy. Who cares if they are intelligent, so long as they are rich? If Henry Ford II had the intellectual capacity of one of Tiffany's lady customers, he would be no less socially acceptable. Only his chauffeur cannot afford to be stupid. Like a millionaire, a woman can take any risk—and it can justly be said that all the risks she takes are sure things—without hurting herself at all. In other words, a woman can be as stupid as she wants to be—in spite of this, a man will take care of her and will not give up her company.

The formula for this female conspiracy could not be simpler: it is masculine to work, feminine to do nothing. And men are so lucky to be men! They are strong and free, while women, weak as they are, are tied to the home by the burden of bearing children. They are simply not made for any valuable kind of work.

Men are so willing to believe this myth that they are even flattered by it. It never occurs to them to think that an elephant is strong, too—stronger than a man, for example. Yet men are better suited to do most jobs than an elephant, in spite of its strength.

Women, of course, will never admit that, in comparison to men, they do nothing; they are constantly finding little tasks and keeping themselves busy. A woman simply tells her husband that her work is of no value compared with his. She implies that all the inane, pointless busywork she indulges in, such as ironing, baking, beautifying the house, all those little jobs that take up her day, is necessary for the family's comfort. He is meant to think himself lucky to have a wife who will perform these menial tasks for his sake. And since men are completely unaware that women actually enjoy such jobs, they *do* think themselves lucky.

Thanks to women, everything is labeled "masculine" or "effeminate," "worthy" or "unworthy." By imbuing all they do with sentimental and emotional values to such a degree that no one can remain unaffected by them, women have created for themselves a fool's paradise. Whatever they do is pointless compared with male achievements. And since they say so themselves, why should men quibble?

Of course, if men really wanted to, they could destroy this tissue of lies and replace the terms "masculine" and "effeminate" with "hard" and "easy." For most work done by men is hard, whereas housework is always easy. With the machines invented for this purpose by men, the work for a household of four persons is easily done in two hours each morning. Anything else a woman chooses to do with her time is superfluous, for her own amusement, and serves to maintain the idiotic status symbols of her clique (lace curtains, flower beds, brilliant polish): if this is called work, then it is nothing more than a shameless, expedient lie.

Housework is so easy that in psychiatric clinics it is traditionally performed by those patients who have become so feebleminded that they are no longer suited to other kinds of work. If women complain that they are not paid extra wages for this work (they demand very little, about the wages of a motor mechanic!), it is only a further proof of how attractive this "work" is to them. Furthermore, such demands are shortsighted, since they may one day lead to an actual evaluation of women as a work force, with commensurate wages. That would reveal to what extent they live, at man's expense, beyond their means.

Still, man has been accustomed to female terminology since childhood, and he has no desire to undermine it. He needs the feeling of doing something great when he supports a woman, he needs to feel a woman could not do his work. Without this conviction, the monotony of his own life would drive him mad. He has only to feel for a second that a woman *could* do his job as well as he can and he will double his own efforts at once. From time to time, as she sees fit, a woman might wish to create this impression, so that the customary distance between himself and the "weaker" sex is maintained and his self-confidence restored.

It is simple to analyze this vicious circle: women invent rules, manipulate men to obey them, and so dominate the male sex. Of course, these rules in no way apply to women themselves. The male sense of honor, for example, is a system invented by women who loudly exempt themselves from it. They renounce the concept of honor and, as a result, manipulate men.

In a recent television series, *The Avengers,* there was a scene in which two antagonists were facing each other across a billiard table, a pistol in front of each of them. It was agreed that to give them each an equal chance, they should count aloud up to three and then shoot. The hero, however, grabbed his pistol and fired at the count of two, thus saving his own life. He chose to remain outside the system and was therefore in a position to manipulate the other who, although in mortal danger, preferred to stick to a system approved by society rather than to use his own judgment.

By making her own work appear degrading and contemptible, woman brings man to the point where he will undertake all the other tasks: in other words, everything she does not want to do. After all, she was there first as his mother, so she has first choice. A man loses his self-respect and feels useless if he has to do "woman's work." In fact, many men are deliberately clumsy at housework—and women love them for it. Such clumsiness is so adorably masculine! If a man is capable of sewing on his own button—and does so—he really is not a "proper" man at all. There must be something wrong with him if he pushes the vacuum cleaner around the house.

Such beliefs enable man to place himself under the guardianship of women; he trusts himself to accomplish almost anything except to make a decent stew. And so he allows himself to be driven away from the most unexacting place of work in the world, without a murmur of complaint. Only after a certain amount of manipulation, when there is no longer any danger, will he be permitted to lend a hand in the house. Even then woman always gives strict orders because he really does not understand about such things. He will always feel vaguely humiliated by a job of this nature and therefore will never notice how much more agreeable it is than his own.

To avoid having to exert effort, all a woman has to do is heave a sigh and indicate that she, "as a woman," is simply not capable of the task. If she merely hints to a man, preferably with witnesses present, that he drives so much better than she does, she has found herself a chauffeur for life. Look at the highways—they are full of women being driven by their husband-chauffeurs. A woman will say that she cannot possibly, "as a woman," go to a café or a theater or a restaurant by herself. There is no rational explanation for this:

No

women are served equally well or badly whether alone or accompanied by men. And if she doesn't want to be accosted, why does she dress to make herself so conspicuous? No, instead she will get herself a flunky, who will drive her to the entrance as if she were royalty, fight for a table, order her dinner, entertain her, and finally pay the bill.

When a woman claims politics are too difficult for her to understand, there will always be a man ready to plow through the newspapers, study political journals, listen to protracted television discussions, sift other men's theories, and, behold, when the time comes to vote, he presents her with an opinion. So, armed with his conclusion as to what is best for his, hence also her, position in life, off she goes to register his choice. In that way the election result is not in jeopardy. The alternative might mean the end of her personal well-being. Although she might not understand what politics are about, she is shrewd enough to realize this.

One of the most fantastic flowers of this manipulation through self-abasement is the life of a well-to-do woman today, living comfortably in some pleasantly situated suburban ranch house. Surrounded by children, dogs, other women, by every possible kind of labor-saving device, equipped with television sets and second cars, she will tell her husband, possibly a lawyer or engineer, what a lucky man he is, what a fulfilled life he leads, while she, "as a woman," is constrained to lead a life unworthy of a human being: she says this to the man who has paid for all that trash with his life, and he believes her.

In the Bible it is said that Eve was created from Adam's rib. She is a copy, therefore a species of a lower order: yet another example of manipulation through self-abasement. Can anyone doubt that at some stage in history this story was invented by a woman? She herself did not write it down, a man did this for her, since her ability to write is a comparatively recent skill.

A Dictionary

CONSTANT SELF-ABASEMENT in the presence of men has led women to develop a secret language which other women understand but is incomprehensible to men, since they take it literally. It would, therefore, be a great advantage to men to hold the key to this code and so create a sort of dictionary for themselves. Then, whenever they heard a standard phrase, they could decipher its real meaning.

Here are a few examples, with a translation into male language.

CODED	DECODED
A man must be able to protect me.	A man must be able to spare me from all forms of discomfort. (What else could he protect her from? Robbers? An atom bomb?)
I need a man to make me feel secure.	Above all, he must keep his money worries to himself.
I must be able to look up to a man.	To be a possible candidate as a husband, he must be more intelligent, responsible, courageous, industrious,

CODED	DECODED
	and stronger than I am. Otherwise. what purpose would he serve?
Of course I would give up my career if my husband asked me.	Once he is earning enough money, I am never going to work again.
The only thing I want in life is to make him happy.	I will do everything in my power to stop him from knowing how much I exploit him.
I will never bother him with trivial problems.	I'll do anything rather than keep him away from his work.
I am there for him alone.	No other man has to work for me.
In future I shall devote my life to my family.	I'm not going to lift another finger for the rest of my life. It's his turn now.
I don't believe in Women's Liberation.	I'm not such a fool. I'd rather let a man do the work for me.
After all, we are living in an age of equality.	If he thinks he can order me about, just because he earns money for me, he is sorely mistaken.
I'm so bad at doing things like that.	That's a job he will have to do. What's he there for, anyway?
He knows absolutely everything.	He even serves the function of an encyclopedia.

CODED	DECODED
If a couple really love each other, there is no need to get married at once.	He is being a bit obstinate, but I'll soon get around him in bed.
I love him.	He is an excellent workhorse.

Of course women use stock phrases like these only when there is a man around to hear them. In the company of other women they talk about their men quite normally, as they would speak of a domestic appliance, which everyone knows to be practical anyway.

If a woman says, "I've decided to give up wearing this coat—or that hat—because my boy friend doesn't like it," she really means, "I might as well do him that favor. He's doing everything I want anyhow."

When women are among themselves, discussing the desirable qualities of a specific man, they will never declare that they want someone to look up to, someone who will protect them. Such twaddle would be greeted with the laughter it deserves. They are more likely to say they want a man with such and such a job: jobs are synonymous with income level, old-age pensions, widows' endowments, and the ability to pay high life-insurance premiums. Or a woman might well say, "The man I'm going to marry must be a little older than I, at least half a head taller, and more intelligent." By which she means that it looks "normal" for a somewhat older, stronger, more intelligent human being to provide for a younger, weaker, more stupid creature.

If women can manipulate men so well, they can't be all that stupid.

49

Women Have No Feelings

Woman has a great many methods to manipulate a man, but to list them all here is impossible. Suffice it to look more closely at two relatively harmless methods: a man's "good manners" and the suppression of his emotions.

Any man who wishes to be a success with women—and is there one who doesn't?—must acquire a variety of qualifications. Apart from intelligence, ambition, industry, and pertinacity, he must know exactly how to behave in the presence of women. With this aim in view, women have established certain norms which are called good manners. Basically the rule is that any man who has a sense of self-respect must, at all times, treat a woman like a queen. Similarly, a self-respecting woman must, at all times, give man every opportunity of treating her like a queen.

A woman will marry a man simply because he is wealthy. But if she is given the choice between two wealthy men, one with and one without manners, she will choose the man who has them. For if a man has mastered the rules governing good manners, a woman may be sure that he will never, at any time, question her ideal value as a woman, which he has long since been conditioned to respect, not even after she has ceased to attract him.

Psychologists state that happiness comes with laughter, faith with prayer. This is true, but only for men. If he treats woman as a superior being, she will become a superior being for him. Women are more gifted to differentiate between fact and fiction. Unlike other methods of manipulation, good manners are not the result of conditioned forms of behavior based on profound psychological motivation. Children are taught "to behave" relatively late, and manners are particularly easy to recognize as a form of women's exploitation. It is a puzzle why even today such old tricks are still successful.

The advice a mother gives to her teenage son going out on his first date is a good example of woman's audacity:

Pay the taxi; get out first; open the door on the girl's side and help her out.

Offer her your arm going up the steps or, if they are crowded, walk behind her in case she stumbles so that you can catch her.

Open the door into the foyer for her; help her out of her coat; take the coat to the cloakroom attendant; get her a program.

Go in front of her when you are taking your seats and clear the way.

Offer her refreshments during the intermissions—and so on.

And on top of that we should not forget that the average type of play is an outdated form of entertainment because most of them are aimed at the intellectual level of women (as, indeed, are many of those things which we like to label "cultured"). Pity the poor man who has to submit to all this. He probably has an inkling that not only he but the assembled company of directors, actors, and producers awaiting them are there only to form the background for woman and her clique. This background is simply a place where she can indulge in her inane orgies, where she and other women can take part in their grotesque masquerades, with the extras, the men, suitably costumed in black.

The most cynical aspect of the "good manners" etiquette is the *role of protector* which is forced on a man. This begins harmlessly enough, it is true. He follows her when going upstairs, or walks on the traffic side of a pavement. It is when we reach the level of military service and war that the significance of this becomes more serious. One of the most important rules is that a man must, under all circumstances, protect a woman from unpleasantness—even, if necessary, with his life. And as soon as he is old enough, he will do just that. This training is accomplished at such an early age that in any catastrophe a man will save women and children before he thinks of himself—at the cost of his own life.

There is no compelling reason why these roles should not be reversed. Since woman is unfeeling, she could cope with the psychological effects of war atrocities more easily than a man, and the modern form of war requires neither physical strength nor intelligence, only the ability to survive (tenacity). All statistics about life-spans show that women live longer than men, and therefore are tougher. A normally developed North American woman who has taken sports at school, for example, is certainly not inferior in physical strength to the much smaller Vietnamese men. A GI fighting against Asian men is making war on an enemy no stronger than his college girl friends.

We have already mentioned woman's *lack of emotional capacity*. The fact that women make every attempt to suppress man's ability to express his emotions is a certain indication of this. Yet she still contrives to create the myth of feminine depth of feeling and vulnerability.

The tear ducts are tiny pouches containing fluid. With training they can be controlled, just as one controls the bladder, so that there is no more need for an adult to cry than there is for him to wet his bed. A male child is taught very early in life to control both these functions. Once again, woman degrades herself. "Boys don't cry! You're not a little girl, dear!" Little girls, on the other hand, are never taught to control their tears, and they quickly learn to use them to advantage. If a man sees a woman crying, it would never occur to him that she may be incontinent. He assumes her feelings are aroused to a considerable extent and even judges the degree of feeling by the quantity of liquid shed.

This is obviously a mistaken interpretation. Women really are callous creatures—mainly because it is to their disadvantage to feel deeply. Feelings might seduce them into choosing a man who is of no use to them, i.e., a man whom they could not manipulate at will. They might even actively come to dislike men (after all, men are beings who should be alien to them) and decide to spend their lives exclusively in the company of women. In fact, however, there are far _fewer_ overtly homosexual women than homosexual men, and such women are generally well-to-do or at least financially secure.

A woman with feelings would have to think and work, to take on responsibilities, and to learn to do without all the things which mean so much to her. Because she does not want this, she decides to remain callous, but she knows, at the same time, that it is necessary for woman to enact the role of a sensitive being or man would become aware of her essentially cold, calculating nature. Still, as her emotions are always faked and never felt, she can keep a clear head. You can take advantage of someone's feelings only if you are not involved yourself. Therefore, she turns her partner's emotions to her own profit, only taking care to make sure he believes she feels as deeply as he himself, perhaps even more deeply. She must make him believe she, "as a woman," is much less stable, much more irrational, much more emotional. Only thus may her deception remain undetected. But manipulation has, in any case, already taken care of that.

A real man does not weep or laugh very loud (reserved smiles have a sympathetic effect on those around him and make him seem a serious person to his business associates); he never shows surprise (he never screams "Ahhh . . . !" when a light goes on nor "Ohhh . . . !" when he touches cold water); he never shows that he is making an effort (by saying "Uff . . . !" when he has lifted a heavy case); he does not even sing when he is happy. Therefore, if a man notices all these emotional reactions in a woman, it never occurs to him that he has been conditioned by a woman not to express his own similar feelings. As a result, he assumes she is much more sensitive than he is, for otherwise she would not dare to exhibit her feelings in such an uncontrolled manner. A man who would cry only if a real catastrophe occurred (perhaps the death of his wife) must assume that when his wife breaks into floods of tears because of cancelled holiday plans, for example, her emotions are equally strong, but for a lesser cause. He even thinks himself loutish and callous because he cannot share her grief. What an advantage a man would have if only he realized the cold, clear thoughts running through a woman's head while her eyes are brimming with tears!

Sex as a Reward

EVERY METHOD OF MANIPULATION is based on the carrot-and-stick principle whose applicability depends to a large extent on the ratio of physical strength possessed by trainer and trainee. When dealing with the young, the carrot is favored as a means of control. It has the advantage of maintaining children's trust in adults so that even at a later date they will bring their problems to their parents—and so the process of manipulation is continued. This is much more effective than to start with the stick.

If a captive dolphin has learned to do a trick well, its trainer throws it a fish. Because the dolphin wants to eat, it will do whatever is asked of it. Man, however, since he earns money, is quite capable of providing his own food. It would be impossible to bribe him in this way. He would, in fact, be above bribery altogether were it rot for one basic male need which has to be satisfied: the need for physical contact with a woman's body. This need is so strong, and its fulfillment gives man such intense pleasure, that one suspects that it may be the prime reason for his voluntary enslavement to woman. His longing for subjection may even be a facet of his sexual make-up.

The basis of any economy is a system of barter. Therefore, someone demanding a service must be able to offer something of equal value in exchange for it. But as a man must fulfill his sexual desires and, since he tends to want to possess exclusive rights over one vagina, the prices have risen to an extortionate level. This has made it possible for women to follow a system of exploitation which puts the most exploitative robber barons to shame. And no man remains exempt. The concept of femininity is essentially sociological, not biological. Even a homosexual is unlikely to escape without paying his dues. The partner whose sexual drive is less developed quickly discovers the weak points of the other, whose drive is more intense, and manipulates him accordingly. It will always be the woman, or the "female" partner in any homosexual relationship, who exploits the man: for to be a female means to be undersexed.

Just as woman denies herself any depth of emotion, she denies herself a sexual appetite: how else can a young girl tell her boy friend she loves him but refuse him her body? Thanks to her mother's advice, a girl will suppress her desires even in puberty for the sake of the capital to be gained later. In earlier societies a bride had to be a virgin to be worth anything, and even today a girl who has little sexual experience will have a higher market value than one who has had a number of lovers.

Chastity in a man, on the other hand, has never been worth much. As women do not really care for men, they are not much interested in their chastity. For this reason a boy can never be raped by an older woman—only seduced. But let a man play that game with an adolescent girl! He will be lynched as a sex criminal by a female mob.

A man could, of course, condition his sexual needs as easily as a woman, provided his training started at a very early age. Sufficient proof of this are the monks, the majority of whom survive without sexual satisfaction (nobody will seriously maintain that they are all eunuchs). But instead of learning to suppress his needs, a man will allow them to be encouraged whenever pos-

The Female Libido

As it is difficult to test or classify the degree to which woman feels sexual stimulation, or to define the exact nature of a female orgasm, men get into considerable difficulties when they try to analyze her capacity for sexual excitability and orgasm. If they make any attempt to come to conclusions on the subject, they are forced to rely to a large extent on the information women volunteer to them. And since women have no respect for exact scientific data and are interested only in what is of immediate benefit to them, they will say what seems to be convenient or opportune at the time. Consequently, any facts acquired on the subject of a woman's reactions—whether, for instance, she is frigid, to what degree she can enjoy sexual intercourse, or whether her own orgasm can be compared to that of a man—tend to be extremely contradictory (it is supposed that even Masters and Johnson did not get an average woman onto their test bed). As a result, man vacillates between the conviction that woman has no true sexual drive and the fear that she is more highly sexed than he is—but refrains from telling him so out of pity. He will spend days working out bigger, better, and subtler questionnaires in his efforts to come to some conclusion. And, in the interests of science, he expects women to answer his questions truthfully. As if she could—or would.

It is probable that the truth lies somewhere between

the two extremes. Certainly women are not all nympho-
maniacs or there would be more male prostitutes. On
the other hand, women do not feel an intense aversion
to sex, as has so often been maintained.

Women live an animal existence. They like eating,
drinking, sleeping—even sex, providing there is nothing
to do and no real effort is required of them. Unlike a
man, a woman will rarely make an effort to get her
partner into bed. If, however, he is already there, and
she hasn't planned to set her hair or undertake some
other form of large-scale beauty repair, and there is no
TV program she wants to see, she will not be averse to
making love, provided he is prepared to be the active
partner. But even the euphemisms "active" for the male
partner and "passive" for the female do not conceal the
fact that woman allows man to serve her in bed just as
he does in every other sphere of her life. Even though
intercourse may give a man pleasure in the long run, it
is nothing more than a service to a woman, in which
the man is the better lover, arousing desire more skillfully, quickly, and making it last longer.

Men suspect that women tend to exploit them during
intercourse and have developed a certain fear of female
sexual appetite. Signs of this appear in the rites of an-
cient cultures, in philosophical works of men such as
Schopenhauer and Nietzsche, in the novels of Balzac or
Montherlant, in plays by Strindberg, O'Neill, Tennessee
Williams. Since the discovery of oral contraceptives,
this fear has reached almost hysterical proportions.
Whole books are devoted to the question whether a
man needs to worry about woman's sexual demands,
and, if so, to what extent—and at the same time, advertising has discovered new opportunities to make
money by selling men advice on how to achieve sexual
dexterity.

In truth, reliable oral contraceptives (invented by a
man, naturally) have robbed man of the only triumph
left to him in his state of sexual subjugation. Previ-

ously, woman was always to a certain extent at his mercy. Now she is suddenly in control. She can have as many children as she wishes. She can even select the father (if possible rich). If she has no intention of having children, she can indulge in intercourse as often as it appears advantageous to her.

Man cannot do that. He had always claimed that his sexual potency was without limit and that he only needed an unreserved woman to prove it. Today this is impossible. Any woman can read for herself in popular magazines exactly how potent men are. She will know how active he will be at any given age, whether his best time is afternoon or night, if he is a better lover before or after a meal, and whether his prowess increases in the mountains or at the seashore. She knows how often he can make love on any one occasion in order to satisfy her. What is more, she can be sure of her statistics, for men would never cheat when giving information of this kind; a masculine man would consider it a sign of weakness to lie in any situation at all. So women can rely absolutely on the figures given and know exactly what a man should be able to achieve. He has provided her with charts to determine any man's potency at any given stage in his life: and, thanks to efficient birth-control methods, she can experiment with different kinds of men and compare their sexual performances. Contrary to men's fear, women do not, however, weigh one man against another and choose the most virile—far from it, as she herself is not all that keen on sex. In view of that, and provided all other conditions are equal, she is likely to prefer the less potent man because she can always blackmail him with her intimate knowledge of his weakness.

In the realm of sex, more than any other, man is a victim of the principles of efficiency according to which he is manipulated. Indeed, he sets his own standards: three times in a row, very good; twice, good; once, satisfactory. If he fails as a sex machine, he is, in his opinion, a total failure. Even if he is a brilliant scientist he will never again be really happy. Women know this and take advantage. For example:

a. She can pretend she is unaware of her husband's lack of virility and continue to praise him for his prowess. (Probably the most frequent method applied.)

b. She can make a man believe his sexual failure is a real handicap, so that he considers himself lucky she stays with him.

c. She can threaten to expose his sexual inadequacy unless he does everything she wants; since a man would rather be called a thief or a murderer than impotent, he will bow his head to his fate and do what he is told.

Man's sexual potency depends on psychological factors more than any other of his bodily functions. Once he has begun to doubt his potency, he gradually finds himself in more and more difficulty. His fears of becoming useless to a woman increase because, as a result of women's manipulation, he identifies his masculinity with his dependence on them. For this reason, he will resort to every possible means to remain dependent. One really should reflect on the absurdity of this situation. Aphrodisiacs, once hidden discreetly under the counter and usually prepared by quacks, have long since become socially acceptable and are among the best-selling products of the pharmaceutical industry. Even in serious publications the number of articles on sexual difficulties is increasing; and men's room jokes, which, as we all know, are the result of man's castration anxiety, are heard more frequently, though they are usually quite humorless. And men certainly do not buy pornographic magazines for pleasure—there are so many better and more sophisticated ways of amusing themselves. Their interest lies solely in the hope of finding, in such powerful stimulation, some means of retaining this mythical level of masculine virility.

All this serves to make man once again the victim of his habit of thinking of women in terms of his own standards. He really believes that women, now safe from the dangers of conception, are thinking about nothing but how to make up for lost time, to spend the rest of their lives making love. This is a natural assumption, since he has been manipulated to think that sex is the height of all pleasure. He is, of course, quite mistaken. A woman will certainly feel happy when she has an orgasm—but it is not the most intense pleasure she knows. A cocktail party, or buying a new pair of aubergine-colored patent-leather boots, rates far higher.

Man's fear of losing ground at the sexual or physical level, as a result of woman's newfound freedom, is, of course, quite absurd. No matter how much a woman enjoys making love, she will never let the man who supports her tire himself so that he might be late to work the next morning. That is too big a risk to take. Even the most passionate woman will reduce her sexual activities if she thinks nights spent in making orgiastic love are beginning to affect his work. Nymphomaniacal women exist almost solely in films and plays. Just because they are so rare in real life, the public is curious about them (for the same reason, so many films and novels are about extremely rich people, who form such a small percentage of the total population).

There is only one aspect of a man's sexual potency that concerns a woman—whether he is capable of fathering children or not. Children, as we shall see later, are essential to a woman if she is to bring her plans to fruition. It is probable that many women would be pleased if man's need for sex dried up after she had produced two or three children. It would do away with numerous small inconveniences.

That sexual competence in a man is a matter of indifference to the majority of females is shown by the number of highly paid men who marry, and stay married, despite the fact that they are impotent (it is inconceivable that a woman without a vagina would have any expectation whatever of marriage to a normally sexed man).

Manipulation Through Bluff

MAN'S STRONG SEXUAL DRIVE, his brilliant mind, and his need for a system that will help him bear those responsibilities recognized by his intelligence have enabled women to make effective use of certain institutions that properly belong to the past—institutions like the Church, the many nonconformist sects, and other religious communities: she cold-bloodedly uses them to help with the manipulation of her children. She exploits their armies of clergymen and other functionaries as a kind of military police force designed to protect women's interests even after her children are grown up. Hence it is advantageous to women, as we have already noted, to be neither religious nor superstitious. Unless a boy's manipulation has been exceptionally successful, as in the case of those who decide to become priests, men are equally unlikely to believe in the dogma of their Church. But if its teachings are inculcated at a very early age, they do help to provide certain archetypes and a useful basis for the standards of good and evil. These are standards which have no rational roots but are part of men's subconscious and are therefore ineradicable. Essentially these standards are always the standards of women.

Any religious system must be based on manipulation since it consists of a series of rules and taboos, with a catalogue of penalties for trespass against those rules. These trespasses are called sins. The penalties for them are never imposed in reality, for faith in some kind of superconsciousness is a system without real foundation. No one could know about secret sins or exact punishment for them. As a result, people are apt to say that an unavoidable misfortune such as the loss of a friend or an earthquake is a punishment. In earlier times, when men's understanding of such disasters as plagues, crop failures, and lightning was limited, men believed they were punishments for sins committed at some previous time. And so they thought to avoid them in the future by unconditional surrender to rules, or by repentance, a kind of brainwashing. Such myths become obvious as man's mind develops. He can prove fallacy by committing a sin without incurring any subsequent signs of wrath. But the deep-seated fear of punishment (the *feeling* of having sinned), carefully cultivated during a child's earliest years, will prevent him, as an adult, from doing something that was considered "bad" when he was a child. And if, by chance, he does do something which as a child he called a sin, he will have at the very least a bad conscience.

One sin which figures in almost all of these catalogues is pleasure in the sexual act when reproduction is not intended. And since men, provoked by women, always take pleasure in sex, they yield to this pleasure as often as possible and never once give a thought to reproduction (during orgasm, man experiences a certain kind of pleasure far from the joy of having just engendered a child—thus in this moment man is even more than ordinarily deluded). They constantly transgress against the rules of their childhood beliefs and thus always carry with them a feeling of sin. Women, on the other hand, having learned to control their sexual urge and to make love for the most part not for their own satisfaction but for some specific purpose (breadwinning, reproduction, gratification of a man—in the latter case, an act of charity), commit no sins thereby; even if they consider sex sinful, they are immune to remorse. Unlike men who are constantly forming new resolutions which they never stick to, women do not have such a debit (or guilt) account in any system made for their use—even if they believed in such a system. With their tendency to self-abasement, their suppressed and stunted sexual needs, their assumption that they will survive without working by letting others work for them, they resemble those figures—Jesus Christ, Gandhi—who allow themselves to be considered ideals by men; ideals, which men because of their slavery to their instincts can never attain, and which confirm their suspicion that all qualities truly worthy of worship are in the last analysis feminine.

Yet, in reality, neither women nor their chosen police force, the clergy, are really interested in man's sexual drive. The taboo did not have to apply to this particular instinct. They merely chose it because it is man's greatest—and purest—pleasure. Had he derived as much satisfaction from smoking or eating pork, woman would have equated smoking or eating pork with sin. The point is to keep him in a state of sin (fear), thus open to manipulation. This is one of the reasons why the catalogue of sins varies according to a man's age. For a small child, the taboo is lying, coveting the property of others, and not honoring one's father and mother. For an adult, it is sexual desire and lusting after one's neighbor's wife.

Yet how can they recognize these sins when they know neither the rules nor the system in whose name they were established? How can they believe in something that does not exist, or feel ashamed of a pleasure that does not hurt anyone? Anything that deals with religious beliefs is contrary to the rules of reason and consequently has to be instilled at an age when a sense of logic is as yet undeveloped. If possible, this should take place in a building whose absurd design and architecture equal the absurdity of that which is preached in it, thus making it all a little less incredible. And the purveyors of this type of illogical thinking should, if possible, look different from other people. If children are taught by men who dress like women, for example, or who adopt some other form of masquerade, their pupils' bewilderment and awe will be all the greater, and their respect for these figures will never entirely leave them.

Women have taken great care to ensure that their lobby, the clergy, are always men. First, because the female image might be damaged if they represented their own interests—men might think them calculating—and second, because they know men rate feminine intelligence rather low, which is why they can only influence a man's emotions. Advice from another man, and one respected from childhood, is much more likely to be listened to and taken. Although this advice always benefits women (for example, they will advise a man to stay with a woman he doesn't love, or support children he never wanted), it does not reflect hostility on the part of this lobby toward "normal" men, but is a direct consequence of that lobby's financial dependence on women.

Women could survive easily without the Church (they only need it for the training of men and children, or as a setting for the display of specialized wardrobes), but the Church would be ruined without the support of women. Children can be trained and today are very often raised without the Church's help. It is entirely possible that women one day might give up the nave of a church as the most effective background for a white dress. They might even consider a registrar sufficient to subdue a nervous bridegroom. Such trends would empty the churches in a couple of years. In the Soviet Union "Marriage Palaces" have taken their place as a wedding background. If this became the fashion, people would see churches for what they really are—relics of a long-dead age. They would withdraw their financial support, both public and private, which in the last analysis has always been provided by men. It is man who pays his own tormentors. So when we hear someone say what magical power the Church has, since it still draws people to it after many hundreds of years, the circumstance has obviously been misunderstood. It is not the Church which possesses a magical power—it is women. All such institutions have long since become mere tools in the hands of women, and it is unlikely that they will ever do anything other than fulfill women's expectations.

Ultimately, the victims are not the representatives of the various religious communities themselves. They want only to live a peaceful, undisturbed life (at the expense of masculine men, of course, just like women) and have become a kind of Mafia used by women to terrify children, enslave men, and put a brake on progress. These men are forced, under the threat of boycott, to appear in ludicrously effeminate clothes, to intone grotesque songs loudly, and to tell horror stories to a sometimes even intelligent audience. All this despite the fact that these stories, by which they make such abject fools of themselves, have long been discarded by modern theology and stand in obvious contrast to all they have been taught as students at their universities.

Modern theology, of course, is useless for conditioning purposes now that it has renounced the carrot-and-stick principle. Women need those moth-eaten tales of heaven and hell, of devils and angels, of paradise and judgment day. Death is only a useful means of manipulation if it is a door leading either to eternal happiness or to eternal damnation. To which of these two realms this door may lead is dependent on a kind of point system, scored according to earthly achievement and calculated by women. If life everlasting can be won only by faithfulness and slavery, it falls in with the interests of women—interests which would in no way be furthered if men decided to investigate eternal life in biological terms, an investigation for which we might have to wait a couple of generations.

Women themselves are, of course, quite unmoved by all these myths. They go to church only if and when they want: their consciences do not bother them either way. For the big ceremonies which are really attempts at intimidation—on the part of women, not on that of clergymen—they array themselves in suitable attire: wedding dresses, christening clothes, mourning clothes, confirmation dresses, their men in the usual dark suits. They enact the roles of believer, superstitious person, or skeptic—but in reality their minds are elsewhere. They are not interested in male speculations on the possibility of walking on water, turning water into wine by magic, or by achieving, also with the help of magic, an immaculate conception. As usual their interest does not concern itself with the essence of the thing as such, but with its possibilities of exploitation. If a man of another faith wants to marry a woman and demands her conversion in exchange for his own promise to work for her, no woman would hesitate for a moment.

Commercialized Prayers

For MOST MEN all that remains of the religious faith of childhood are a few conditioned behavioral reflexes, such as a *love of truth,* the *enjoyment of honest, hard work,* or a *pleasure in non-freedom.*

From the moral point of view, everyone should have the right to lie. It helps us to stave off society's often too bold attempts to supervise us and thus minimize our own personal fight for existence. The disadvantage of lying is that if everyone does it, it loses its usefulness. If anyone is gullible enough to believe something that is not true, he must himself love the truth and assume a similar love in others. Consequently, a lie becomes a luxury: it has rarity value. The rarity value has to be maintained by incessant denigration, in the interest of liars. Therefore, it is very important that women teach men love of truth: for only if he loves truth, is she able to afford the luxury of lying.

For contemporary society to survive at all, men must believe in truth. They do the work, and no practical, i.e., logical, system can function on lies. In the highly developed system of contemporary society, where all labor is divided, each man must be able to work with, and rely on, the other. If men were to take to lying when the moment seemed opportune, say in matters such as train schedules, freighters' capacities, or the amount of fuel left in an airplane's tank, the effect on our commercial system would be disastrous. Within a very short time there would be complete chaos.

Women, however, can lie with a clear conscience. They are not involved in the process of work, so their lies will harm only one person—usually the husband. And, if it is not discovered, it is not a lie at all—it is "feminine guile." The only crime that does not come under this heading is physical unfaithfulness, which a man will not forgive. As a man has been conditioned by women's self-abasement, it seems natural to him that she should use guile, weak and dependent creature that she is, as the only way in which she can hope to guide this powerful, sex-obsessed giant, this unfortunate, wretched "animal." It is no wonder that women, having proved guile a success, talk quite openly about it. You will read about it in one of their favorite media, women's magazines. Mothers hand it out as advice to their daughters. Why not? It is quite justified, since all their comfort depends on it, for they are frequently forced to exploit the same man, first the mother's husband and later, perhaps, if the mother lives under the same roof, the daughter's husband. After all, their whole future comfort depends on whether he comes to heel.

Of course, women would never openly forbid a man to lie. They simply associate lying with repugnance. This is easily done by means of the chosen system of religious faith which connects lying with the idea of fictional punishment, or by a kind of personal magic. If a mother tells her child not to lie to her because it is "bad," he will automatically have a guilty conscience if he does. She does not even need to be specific about this "badness." The child believes her implicitly, is dependent on her, and relies upon what she tells him. He believes she would never lie. This is nonsense, of course, for mothers constantly tell their children the most barefaced lies.

The same magic is involved when, later on, a woman convinces her husband that unfaithfulness is something squalid and wretched: "You must never deceive me," or if she happens to be one of those "tolerant" wives: "It's not so bad if you deceive me, but you must never, under any circumstances, leave me." A generous woman! And he will obey her order, for such it is, without doubting its justification. Once in a while he will sleep with another woman, but he will rarely leave his wife, although her admission of boundless indifference should be a signal to him to leave her at once!

Only one circumstance in a man's life will ever make him tell a lie and that is when he, as a result of pent-up desire, has slept with another woman, although he dearly loves his own wife. He is so afraid of the possible consequences (she might do the same thing herself!) that he will suffer the most agonizing pangs of conscience rather than admit the truth. But if he has merely smashed up the car and maybe even killed someone in the process, if he has behaved treacherously toward someone else, or taken a day off from work, he would rather clear his conscience and tell her.

A woman's reactions are exactly the opposite. She will keep quiet about absolutely everything except her interest in another man or that man's interest in her; if two or three other men are attracted, she will use the situation to her advantage by advertising it at once. She tells her husband just to make sure he knows there is someone else to look after her if necessary. This alone is enough to shape a man up and increase his rate of output immediately.

We have already mentioned man's desire to be unfree. This leads to religious fervor and prayer, a fact which is still true today, for pop songs are only a modified version of childhood prayers. The god of former days has been conveniently replaced by the goddess, woman, who is right at hand. Man's happiness really does depend on woman. Even the content of the prayers remains virtually the same: the longing to submit oneself to a higher power, a plea for her to listen to him and be merciful, or simple idealization. It doesn't matter whether one says, "So take my hands . . ." or "And thy right hand shall hold me . . ." or "Fly me to the moon . . ." It all amounts to the same in the end. Some modern records do still praise the old god, but only the choice of words shows they are not directly referring to women: "Thou who makest all things grow . . ."

Prayers and religious songs, i.e., prayers to music, ease existential anxiety. They appeal to a superego on whose every whim happiness depends. This superego allows us to relax and accept life, and frees us from the pursuit of happiness, for everything lies in the hands of our god. As man grows older, his fear increases. He has come to realize why it is justified, and, increasingly, his wish to let go grows too, this need to relax for a few moments at least and to commit himself to this almighty power. In the old days intellectual men used to work out their fears by writing love poems which took the place of prayer and calmed them down. Nowadays this form of adoration has become superfluous; the current supply of pop songs—the dark longings of men, naturally commercialized at their own expense—increases, and their lyrics, for example those of the Beatles, satisfy the most sophisticated of tastes.

There are, of course, also some hits sung specifically in praise of men. Those few are usually songs first made popular by a male singer and then sung by a woman. In general, however, women only sing hymns to love which, since men need them for love, is almost the same as singing hymns to themselves. Still, at some stage they discovered that they could sing their own praises without being too obvious, and ever since women have ceased to worry. They praise their own magnificence, their fickleness, their cruelty, and the self-complacency with which they give themselves to men—whether to save or destroy them.

When Marlene Dietrich sang in *The Blue Angel* that "love is my world and my nature and nothing else," "all I can do is make love that's all," and "men flutter

around me like moths and burn up and I can't help it,"
she was expressing just these sentiments. If women can
think of themselves as divine, just how divine must
they be!

In real life, of course, women are far more subtle in
their exploitation of the male sex than in that film.
They don't ruin men immediately—they are quite
prepared to take a whole lifetime over it. After all, who
is going to kill the goose that lays so many golden eggs?
That is why men were able to laugh over the wretched
figure of Professor Unrath instead of recognizing in him
a portrait of themselves.

Think of Nancy Sinatra's great hit, which says the
same in a slightly different way:

> *These boots are made for walking*
> *'n that's just what they'll do*
> *One of these days*
> *these boots are gonna walk all over you**

A hit indeed—for it satisfies man's need and longing
for a cruel goddess on the one hand—and woman's
claim to omnipotence on the other.

---

* Copyright © 1965 Criterion Music Corp.

Self-Conditioning

THE IDEAL OF ANY TRAINER would be to bring an animal to a level where it is capable of training itself. This is something which still has to be achieved. But man is not an animal, and there comes a point when he does continue his own training, because he is much more intelligent than his female trainer. This will work only as long as he never forgets the purpose of his education and keeps both reward and punishment in mind at all times.

The world of pop songs is one example of man's efforts at self-manipulation. The best example of self-conditioning, however, is to be found in the *advertising industry*. In advertising man does not idealize woman from any masochist tendency. It is purely a question of survival. Only his exploiters, women, have sufficient time and money to buy and consume all his products. To supply the woman inhabiting his ranch house with purchasing power, he has no choice but to cultivate legions of other women who have as much satisfaction as his own wife in spending. They will then buy his goods and keep his wife in pocket money. This is the beginning of a vicious circle—a vicious circle which turns faster and faster until he cannot keep up with it anymore and someone else has to take over. There is no getting off and running away.

Market-research institutes investigate what they like to call subliminal female stimuli (the conscious ones have long since been satisfied) and then sell their discoveries to manufacturers. The latter then hurry to fill these so-called gaps in the consumer market, as if there were in fact such things. Or sometimes they work in reverse. The producer invents a new article which he believes might appeal to women and then hires an advertising agency to create the necessary consumer interest—sometimes with success, sometimes without. The American craze for prefabricated houses, for example, has not caught on to a large extent in any of the European countries.

Every few years a wave of indignation sweeps over the male ranks as a result of this expensive fostering of the female craze for consumption. They have been blinded by the stereotyped image of woman as victim of male exploitation to such an extent that they do not realize that they themselves are, in fact, the sufferers. They maintain that women's naïveté and their gullible, i.e., "stupid" natures are exploited by advertisers for the purpose of increasing sales. One day these men will get around to asking themselves who is really being exploited. Is it the creature whose innermost wishes are sought out, coddled, and fulfilled, or is it he who in his desire to retain the affections of the woman seeks out, coddles, and fulfills them? It has always been one of man's greatest aims in life to fulfill woman's innermost desires, in fact to anticipate her every wish, as contemporary women's fiction still puts it. They have achieved their goal: there is practically no female desire left undiscovered and probably very few which could not, if necessary, be fulfilled.

The result is that women are getting increasingly more stupid, while men grow more and more intelligent. The gap between the sexes is widening constantly, making mutual understanding virtually impossible. But no one seems to notice.

One of the basic principles of biology is that intelligence develops only in the face of competitive stimulation. Women, however, stand outside every competitive field. The glut of modern conveniences dulls their brains, reducing what little is left of their capacity for thought. Man, on the other hand, prodded by the need to create this comfort, to open up new sources of income, has to exert himself more and more.

Surrounded by this ever-increasing comfort, the female sex is changing for the worse. The concept of femininity used to be applied to a woman who had the ability to bear children. It was also applied to venality. The definition must be enlarged to include imbecility.

If Marx is right and the word "being" determines the extent of man's "being aware," the pill, for instance, would determine sexual mores and the atom bomb would stalemate the ideologies of peace; to the same extent the self-awareness of Western woman, whose situation in life has changed ("improved") basically over the last twenty years, is now in a state of acute transformation. This metamorphosis, which can only result in the utter stultification of woman, is all the more dangerous because no one seems to have noticed it. Woman's image is no longer created by woman but by advertising—that is, by man—and if anyone even starts to doubt the truth of woman's value, then there are a hundred snappy advertising slogans ready at hand to disprove such a thought. Advertising says that woman is witty, intelligent, creative, imaginative, warmhearted, practical, and capable. Smiling sweetly, with all the airs of a goddess, she dispenses the latest discovery in instant drinks to her grateful brood. Her husband's eyes follow her adoringly as she serves up a new precooked meal, which is so much more to his taste. Or maybe she hands him a Turkish towel which is even softer than usual—the result of a new rinse. This image of woman, created by man in order to sell his goods, is repeated incessantly with the help of mass media throughout the Western hemisphere; and each day it is being reinforced. How could anyone dare to admit, even to himself, that in reality women are unimaginative, stupid, and insensitive? It would obviously be too much to expect of women—and it is an admission men cannot afford.

Woman buys, man sells. But one does not convince a customer by saying, "It's good. You've got to buy it." Instead we say, "You're marvelous! You deserve the best. Why should you make do with anything less? You've earned your comfort—you are entitled to it!" So, on top of everything else, man has to flatter woman because he needs her as a customer.

It is striking that the trick men are using here appears similar to the one used by women to train men. But, sadly, it is not, since man turns it against himself. She praises him to get him to work for her, but he praises her to make her spend his money. If a man flatters and talks his neighbor's wife into buying new wall-to-wall carpeting for her living room, he must realize that this same neighbor will sell his own wife a bathtub the next day. How else could he pay for the carpeting?

Man is caught in a trap of his own making. While outside the struggle for money is becoming fiercer and fiercer, at home his wife is growing more moronic, and from day to day his house fills up with more junk and knickknacks, thereby financing the stultification of her husband's competitors' wives. Men, who in fact prefer the plain and functional, every day find themselves more deeply entangled in the undergrowth of superfluous ornamentation and all kinds of embellishments. In their living rooms the porcelain cats, barstools, glass-topped tables, candelabra, and silk cushions pile up; in their bedrooms the walls are papered with floral patterns; in their cabinets a dozen different kinds of glasses are lined up; and if they look for a place to put their razors in the bathroom, all the shelves are filled with the thousand creams and cosmetics of their artfully made-up wives.

It is interesting that nearly the only products sold are those of benefit to women: sports cars (with which to entice her), luxury goods (for women), or household appliances (also for women, since the house actually belongs to her—man is, in fact, a homeless creature, moving constantly between office and house). Women would be delighted to buy things for their husbands for whatever occasion, using the latter's money of course (they give ties, sport shirts, ashtrays, wallets, as often as possible). The problem is that a man needs so very little: his clothing is standardized, hence inexpensive; his consumption of food and drink is restricted in case it affects his work capacity; and he has no time to consume other goods—except cigarettes, which he smokes at work.

Industry has made every effort to get men interested in after-shave lotions, hair sprays, or gaily colored leisure wear, but usually in vain. Only young men will take to the latest short-lived fashion: their earning potential, however, is too low to interest women. Rich men, whom women "love" anyway, and artists, who act as a kind of court jester to them, are allowed to sport the latest "in" clothes, and queers, maybe—but not the average man.

Another example of this is Father's Day, which is still not very popular in spite of all the advertising, whereas Mother's Day is a bonanza for everyone concerned. The best thing men can do on their day of celebration is retire to a bar and have a few beers in peace.

Apart from eating, drinking, and smoking, sex is the only activity where man is an independent consumer: he must be able to satisfy his sexual urge. No wonder whole branches of industry are given over to this trade, taking advantage of this need to make him even more lustful and to persuade him to buy goods which merely serve to increase his desire. Satisfaction, of course, is another matter. That has to be had from a woman at the customary price.

As such firms are usually run by men, in order to live a man finds himself in the embarrassing position of having to make lechers of his fellow males. He caters to male desire for women in every conceivable way and proceeds much like Alexander Pavlov and his dog, establishing conditioned reflexes. Pavlov made his dog's mouth water merely by ringing a bell which meant "dinner." In this case, man encourages his fellow men to get an erection by producing photos of half-naked breasts, by means of a suggestive sigh in a popular song, perhaps, or by writing a certain sentence in a book.

That is why man will invent a whole range of methods of obtaining an erection, which another man will have to pay for. And of course, this mechanism does not bring returns only to manufacturers of erotica. All other industries take advantage of it, too. Presents for women are sold to men by means of a picture of an attractive female bosom. A man will read a book or see a movie because he hopes it will give him a kick. And, as a secondary effect, he may suddenly feel the desire to go around the world with his woman, to buy a weekend cottage in the mountains, or to get a sports car.

The American men's magazine *Playboy* provides us with one of the best proofs of man's methods of self-conditioning. Sandwiched between wonderful pairs of naked breasts are excellent articles of a highly theoretical nature to entertain him and to offer him respite between erections; all of this is padded with offers of expensive cars, liquor, unnecessary clothing, and smoker's accessories.

Women are highly offended by magazines like these. But men have lost all sense of the grotesque in this situation. The cult of the bosom has become something quite independent and depersonalized. The sex industry has told men so often and so successfully that women's breasts are there to attract him, that he has quite forgotten their real purpose. The diversion was entirely successful: as a result of the invention of substitutes for mother's milk, he rarely has a chance to watch a baby feed at its mother's breast.

Children as Hostages

CHILDREN ARE endearing, which in itself is no reason for producing them. The creation of a child is in effect the creation of an adult—man or woman. Most adult men live in a state of permanent hell. And the happiness of most women is not only primitive but obtained mostly at other people's expense, so that there is no justification for reproducing them.

It would be mistaken to maintain that only women are interested in having children. Men want them, too. Children are one of the two or three excuses by which they justify their subjection to women. Women, on the other hand, need children to justify their laziness, stupidity, and lack of responsibility. Both sexes exploit the child, therefore, for their own ends.

Although the whole world is full of half-starved orphans, every couple produces its own brood. Man must have a reason to be enslaved when, later on, his sexual powers have declined, and this reason must also explain his enslavement to a particular woman. This is simple. She is, after all, the mother of *his* children. Since woman is the excuse for his subjugation, he can have only one at a time (in every industrial society, man is monotheistic—i.e., monogamous); more than one god (woman) would make him insecure, lead him to question his own identity, and throw him back into the state of freedom he is constantly trying to escape.

Questions such as this do not interest woman. As she

does not think abstractly, the problems of existential anxiety do not touch her. She has no need for a deity to give meaning to her life. All she needs is an excuse for making one particular man work for her long after he ceases to want to go to bed with her. This excuse is provided by bearing his children. If men outnumbered women three to one, a woman would not hesitate to have a child by each of three men and let each of them work for his own child, that is, for her, and play the three men off against each other. Their achievements—and her comfort—would thereby be enormously increased. It is a popular misconception that woman is less inclined to polygamy than man.

When a man engenders children, he gives a woman hostages in hopes that she will exploit him forever. It is the only thing that gives him some sort of stability, and the only way of justifying the senseless slavery to which he has been conditioned. When he works for his wife and child, it is less important that he is supporting two particular human beings who do not look after themselves (one will not because she is female, and the other cannot because he is too small): he is working for a *system* which embraces everything in this world that is poor, helpless, and in need of protection (poor, helpless, and in need of protection *as such*) and which, so he believes, really needs him.

Thanks to wife and child, man has acquired an excuse, an artificial justification for his wretched existence, for his subjection. He calls this arbitrarily created system, this holy unit, his "family." Woman accepts his services in the name of the "family," accepts the hostages he entrusts to her, and proceeds to carry out his desires by binding him ever more tightly to her and blackmailing him until he dies. And whose is the gain?—hers.

Both man and woman only stand to gain by having children—otherwise they would not produce them. Man's advantage lies in the fact that he appears to lead a more meaningful life and that he is able to become a slave forever—and woman has all the other advantages. These must be considerable, for any female today has the choice between a professional life or having children, and nearly all of them choose children.

This may suggest that women decide in favor of a home and family simply because they love children. But women are not capable of the unconditional love a child should have. This can easily be proved. Women only care for their own children, never those of others. A woman will accept a child who is not her flesh and blood only when she is physically incapable of having her own (and this only after everything has been tried—including artificial insemination by an unknown donor).

Although orphanages throughout the world are full of appealing, needy children, and although the newspapers and TV report daily on the number of little Africans, Indians, or South Americans who are starving to death, a woman would rather give a stray dog or cat a home than a deserted child. And yet she pretends to *love* children.

Any news magazine will give the figures on the high rate of abnormal births every year (one in sixty—children with water on the brain, with missing limbs, blind, deaf, or feebleminded), but women are not deterred, and—as if in the grip of an evil spell—they go on producing them one after the other. If a woman gives birth to a deformed or Mongol child, she never feels that her egoism is finally unmasked, that she must take full responsibility for the disaster. As the mother of a feebleminded child, she will be treated as if she were a martyr, respected and admired. And if she doesn't have one already, she will have another child as soon as possible, a "normal" baby, like the babies of other women, to prove that she herself is healthy. She would never think that she is forcing this second, healthy child to spend his whole youth, his whole life, in the company of a moron.

It is difficult to prove that women do not really love

children, that they use them only to their own advantage. After all, pregnancy, childbirth, and the care of an infant are not without some degree of unpleasantness and discomfort. Such factors are unimportant, however, when one considers what a woman is getting in exchange: lifelong security, comfort, and freedom from responsibility. What would a man have to do to achieve a situation vaguely resembling a woman's state?

That pregnancy is not as unpleasant as it is made out to be has by now reached even the ears of men. Many women feel healthier when expecting a child, and it is becoming fashionable to admit it openly. Why should they worry if they look ugly and unattractive, their figures lumpy, skin spotty, hair stringy, and legs swollen? They are not after a man now. They already have one. He, of course, has no choice but to watch his butterfly turn into a caterpillar. He did it, after all! It is *his* child she is expecting, *his* child who is deforming her. What right has he to find her clumsy and repulsive? And, after all, she is losing her youth because of him.

As far as giving birth itself is concerned, the fantasies still surrounding it are so hair-raising that it would never occur to man that women bear children for their own sake and not for his. The phrase, "she presented him with a child," so popular in the novels of previous centuries, may well have gone out of use in contemporary literature. But it has been fixed in the consciousness of men, and when the offspring arrives they are filled with feelings of guilt because of the sufferings of the woman (not those of the newborn infant, please note).

Yet a man only has to imagine that, in return for spending six hours at the dentist, he will be offered a sinecure for life: he would certainly accept such an offer. Of course, difficult births do occur, but they are as a rule painless since the advent of anesthetics. In general, a woman suffers no more during childbirth than she would during a prolonged session at the dentist. What women tell men about giving birth is usually shamelessly exaggerated. The ear-splitting shrieks from the delivery rooms which penetrate their ears are no more than a sign of the same lack of self-control and pride that we have already dealt with at length elsewhere. Painless birth has existed for years. By doing exercises women can train themselves to have their children without anesthetics or discomfort. It would be to women's advantage to decide whether or not having a child is painful. As long as some say one thing and others something else, they lose credibility and thus damage their common interest.

Of course, an assumed air of helplessness and a subsequent excuse for spending their lives doing easy work without a boss ordering them around is not the only reason why women produce little human beings. One day, for example, a woman may discover that her body functions rather like a slot machine. You put in something insignificant and trifling, and something different and fabulous falls out. Of course she is tempted to try this wonderful game. And when she has played it once, she will repeat it over and over again. It nearly always works: exactly nine months later out comes a human being. She is astonished and delighted. The operation of this slot machine is fundamentally as legitimate as when a person hits another on the head (and the latter immediately collapses), simply because it is biologically possible. If each game with her body slot machine did not involve some future effort, she would soon become insatiable. So she draws the line: at the point where one more child would increase her work load and decrease her security and comfort.

As a rule this limit is easily determined—usually by the degree of automation in any one household. In highly industrialized countries, the average woman aims at having two or three children. In North America, where housework is almost wholly automated, the optimum is nearer three. In Western Europe (where certain appliances are not yet used) the ideal is nearer two. An only child is seldom desirable, and more than three are considered antisocial because of their noise and the smell of washing.

An only child affords no benefits, only disadvantages. The woman never seems as unprotected and tied to her home as she should be. Apart from that, something might happen to the child, possibly when the mother is past child-bearing age. Then she would have no excuse left for having things made comfortable for her, and her husband would have no reason to go on working for her alone. Also, an only child has no playmate, and the mother would have to play with him; if there is anything a woman loathes, it is having to play with children. Children are curious about absolutely everything, but a woman has no interests at all except the few idiotic forms of entertainment offered by her house and her own body. With the best will in the world, it is difficult for a mother to enter into the adventurous world of a child. She may have a small repertoire of insipid stock phrases to amuse a toddler ("look who's coming now"), but by the age of two a child has started to think for himself and woman is left behind. The cliché about the common interests of father and son (father cannot stop playing with his son's model railway) cannot be applied to mother and son, or even to mother and daughter. If a woman makes an effort and spends half an hour playing with her child (more might stunt its mental development), she tells the whole world, as if it were a great achievement, which of course it is, in terms of self-denial.

To guarantee material security and allow a woman to seem helpless and incapable of earning a living, two to three children are necessary. This minimizes the risk of old age without children or grandchildren who prove their respect and love, their gratitude to her for being such a good mother and grandmother. Besides, the children keep each other amused, leaving mother free for "superior" occupations, sewing, for example, or baking. Her maternal care consists of locking the children in a room together and coming in only when one of them gets hurt and screams loud enough to summon her.

It follows that raising and training two or more children is much easier than bringing up one. To instill obedience into an only child, the mother has to evolve complex methods to outsmart and persuade it, and get it to see reason; or it has to be punished. Since this is a nuisance, mother usually leaves it to father. Several children, on the other hand, can be trained by emotional blackmail. As they are all dependent on their mother's approval, she has only to show a slight preference for one and the others will do anything she tells them to. Every child lives in constant fear that its mother will "withdraw" her love and give it to someone else. And if this fear does not create affection between siblings (as if woman would care!), it at least increases their competitiveness and performance. Even later, when the children have long since grown up, they will still vie with each other for their mother's respect. The sons satisfy their ambitions in their work, the daughters in the amassing of property. From time to time they all gather together and return to mother. Mother, of course, regards this as a sign of their affection and likes to call the interest her children take in each other's progress "a sense of family." On such occasions each renders an accounting of his or her latest acquisitions.

But all these advantages hold true when there are only two or three children. A woman with more than three, usually because of an oversight on her part or religious beliefs on her husband's, will have plenty to occupy her for a few years, even with the freedom to organize her own timetable and without the responsibility of earning their daily bread. A sense of responsibility as far as the children are concerned is, in any case, alien to woman. The increased activity only lasts until the youngest child reaches nursery-school age. There is, however, one further small advantage in having a large family—the husband is unlikely to leave before all the children are grown up. A man who leaves his wife with four or more children, even if he cannot stand the sight of her a moment longer, is considered almost a criminal in our society.

However, by the time the children have started school, most of even a prolific woman's work is done. Once again she has time and money enough to enjoy herself to a certain extent. She will go to the hairdresser, arrange flowers in vases, paint her furniture according to the latest suggestions in women's magazines, and care for her valuable body. In most Western countries, school lasts all day, and in the few places where it does not, men are busying themselves with their customary vigor to change the system. They have established through their research that children who are not exposed to the influence of their mothers for half a day can develop their mental faculties faster and therefore are capable of greater achievements later on. The practical application of this discovery, which women do not consider at all humiliating—after all, they lack man's sense of honor and therefore cannot be offended in this way—is therefore doubly in their own interest.

Women's Vices

A PILE OF LINEN, neatly ironed, lies in the closet. The roast is nicely browned all over. A curl falls in exactly the right place over the forehead. The pink of the nail varnish matches exactly the pink of the lipstick. The laundry, clean and fresh, is fluttering in the breeze. Ten pairs of shoes stand clean and shiny in a row. The windows are polished till they make the passersby blink. Husband went off to work on time. The children are playing in the sun. Everything is perfect, and woman's world is one hundred percent in order. At such time their sense of pleasure and happiness reaches its zenith. And just to make sure this exhilaration lasts, a woman will quickly bake another cake, water the rubber plant near the living-room window, or get on with knitting a sweater for her youngest child.

Those who do not work have very different pleasures from those who do. A woman does not laze around on a couch surrounded by newspapers. Man's idea of idleness is quite different (and that is why she appears so industrious to him). A woman does not want to stay at home just to rest (what has she, after all, to rest from?)—but she is addicted to pleasure, and she needs time for her pleasures. And what are they? Baking cakes, ironing the laundry, making clothes, cleaning windows, curling her hair, painting her toenails, and sometimes even—and we will come to this later—doing a little shorthand and typing. And just to make sure that no one recognizes the fact that for her all this is pleasure, she calls these pleasures "housework." She is only indulging in orgies of "personal hygiene" to please her partner. And if one of her silly little pleasures is to sit at a desk in an outer office, translating ready-made thoughts (ready-made since they are provided by professional men) into a visual medium, well, let her call it "stimulating mental work." In this way woman and her coterie indulge in a great, permanent party and live in a world of freedom and rationalized happiness, removed from any responsibility. They occupy a realm man would never dare to dream of, a world he believes to be the domain of hippies, a life to be found, perhaps, in the carefree South Sea Islands—but never so close to home.

Of course, there would be nothing to object to in these harmless orgies of pleasure if only men recognized them for what they really are. But it is a pity that they ruin their own lives believing that women's lot is worse. It is quite impossible for a man to imagine that this represents happiness to the opposite sex. They would have to realize that it is woman's nature to be able to enjoy amusements at the lowest and most monotonous level, and such boundless idiocy is beyond male comprehension.

Not even psychologists can grasp it, although they spend their lives studying the female mind. Being men, they must find it more interesting than their own. But it would never occur to them for a minute that woman's so-called psyche is unfathomable merely because of the absence of intelligence; that feminine work appears unattractive to the male only because he is incapable of imagining the required degree of stupidity necessary to be able to enjoy it.

These experts have discovered that most schoolgirls do well in subjects that do not require thought, that can be memorized, such as languages (to have a good memory can, as is well known, also be a sign of feeblemindedness) or that, like mathematics, follow strict rules,

But boys do better in math

which again are learned by rote, while other subjects (physics, chemistry, biology) are beyond them. From this it does not follow that these girls lack intelligence but that there is a "typical feminine" intelligence; that this kind of "intelligence" is a developed (not innate) kind of stupidity. The last original thought the average female child utters will be around age five. After that, her completely imbecile mother takes care to suppress any sign of budding intelligence.

Most men will never admit the depth of their wives' stupidity. They agree that women are not terribly clever, but grant them "intuition" or instinct instead. And they like to call this a feminine instinct as opposed to that of an animal. Unfortunately, this famous feminine instinct is really nothing but a euphemism for statistical probability. Women interfere and give opinions about everything, and, since they are so stupid, they don't realize that they are making fools of themselves. According to the law of averages, their forecasts will be correct now and again. In any case, most of their predictions are negative or vague. Banalities such as: "It can only end in disaster," or "I'd steer clear of that, if I were you," or "Your so-called friends will only let you down in the end" are meaningless. Anyone would be safe making such generalizations. And if, occasionally, women do see more clearly than men, it is only because their feelings, unlike those of men, are never involved.

Women's silliness is but the natural result of their attitude to life. By the age of five, any girl will have been persuaded that she wants to get married and have a home and children; and when girls are ten, fifteen, or twenty, they still want the same things. So if a woman decides, even as a child, to live at man's expense, what good will intelligence and reasoning be to her? She must keep her mind free for her future man, otherwise she could not respond to all his inclinations and interests and praise him for them. As a child, how can she determine what type of man she will marry? What use would it be if she opted to become a socialist—demonstrating female students are usually associated with demonstrating male students—when later on she might decide to marry a well-to-do manufacturer? Suppose she became a vegetarian (sensitive being that she is)—what happens if she later marries an Australian cattle farmer? What is the use of a woman becoming an atheist when she may spend her life within the rose-covered walls of a vicarage?

Would it have helped Jacqueline Bouvier to have developed ideological concepts as an adolescent? A leaning toward democracy helped her first marriage with J.F.K., a leaning toward fascism helps the second. But since she is one of the most "feminine" of women, she is probably not interested in men's beliefs anyway. Basically she is interested only in pleasing and influencing women.

In the end it is probably better if a future lady of society has a smattering of the arts, table manners, and languages so that if she is later in the awkward position of having to play a role in public life—as the wife of a man who plays a role in public life—she can easily get out of her dilemma. All she has to affirm is that a "real" woman's place is in the home, looking after husband and children, and the world will then accept her attitude as one of remarkable self-effacement and applaud her for it.

Women's stupidity is so overwhelming that anyone who comes into contact with it will become, in a way, infected by it. That this is not obvious is solely because everybody has been exposed to it from birth and, as a result, has become inured to it. In previous years men either ignored it or believed it to be a typically feminine characteristic which harmed no one. But with the increase in leisure and money to spend, woman's need for entertainment has grown. Consequently, her imbecility is spreading into public life as well, reflected not just in vases, bedroom pictures, brocade curtains, cocktail parties, and Sunday sermons. The mass media have become more involved in it. Women's programs are gaining ground in radio and television. And even respectable newspapers print society gossip, crime features, and fashion news, horoscopes, and cooking recipes. And women's magazines become every day more numerous and sumptuous on the stands. Step by step, not only the private sphere of men but all of public life has become infected by this stupidity.

There are periodicals and books which deal with politics, philosophy, science, economics, and psychology. There are also those dealing with fashion, cosmetics, interior decoration, society gossip, cookery, crime, and love affairs. Men read almost exclusively the first kind, women exclusively the second. Both groups consider each other's reading matter so repulsive and dreary that they would rather be bored to death than indulge in it. The fact is, men are more interested in whether there is life on Mars or whose arguments are more valid in the Sino-Russian frontier dispute than women are. Women only want to know how to embroider little brown bunny-rabbits, how to crochet a dress, or whether a certain film star is getting a divorce. So the sexes continue along their separate paths, each with his own horizon, never establishing real contact with the other. There is only one subject which will arouse the interest of both, and that is the subject of women.

Naturally some men are not spared the task of reading special women's publications. Although fashion does not interest most men, it is designed chiefly by male slaves: and yet women have the nerve to say they bow to the dictates of the great couturiers. Men also think up other media for female pastimes. In order to be sure such efforts will be a success, they have to lower themselves to women's mental level to find out what they like. Since this is nearly impossible for men, they rely very often on a staff of female editors, who are quite happy to tell them what a woman likes—but from then on it is the man's responsibility; his tasks will be an attractive layout, better distribution, and sales promotion.

Magazines serve many purposes in the female world. Some are for entertainment (for example, *Ladies' Home Journal* and *McCall's*); others satisfy the craving for gossip (*Photoplay* and *Movie Life*); still others give advice on which mask to choose (*Vogue* and *Harper's Bazaar*). There are even magazines which unite the various spheres of interest (such as *Cosmopolitan, Mademoiselle,* and, in Europe, *Elle*). All these magazines have one thing in common: they ignore men. The subject of men's magazines, on the other hand, is almost exclusively women. If man is mentioned at all in a woman's publication, it is only to enumerate his supposed preferences in women, home, and food: "Wear flesh-colored underwear this summer—men love it"; "Natural make-up is preferable for your first date"; "Use candlelight—it makes him feel romantic"; "Three recipes to make him love you"—and so on. And because such wholesale lists of male preferences can only serve to help women catch and hold any given man, they are really no more than recipes. Readers of such advice are either still unmarried and therefore shopping for a good worker, or they are married and thus dependent on keeping what they have already conquered in the way of manpower. These are directives telling women how to get the best out of the most reliable robots in the world, for that is how they regard men. It is not uncommon to see an article entitled "How to Catch Mr. Right," "Ten Hints on How to Keep Him in a Good Mood," and "Advice for the First Three Years of Married Life." There is nothing oblique about articles of this kind: they are as clear and lucid as if they were tips about buying a car, or washing and caring for a cashmere sweater.

Since the range of subjects likely to interest women is necessarily limited, editors are frequently at a loss for copy. As a result they have to fall back on the so-called male themes and, since men's interests are so wide, there are plenty of them. These go through a complete metamorphosis to suit female readers, the main rule of which is quite simple: each article must create the impression that it is basically a report about women. For example, an account of the life of a former heavyweight champion must read: "Women ruined me." If a composer is interviewed for an article, he must say at least once that women are his inspiration, that a melody is "like a pretty girl"—only not quite so beautiful. With skill, even the most unlikely subjects can be camouflaged to appeal to women. One can arouse their interest in the defense budget, providing one dresses up the report as an account of the family life of the Secretary of Defense. It goes without saying that sufficient space must be allowed for pictures of his wife and children. Women will read articles on foreign countries if the passage begins: "I married an Israeli" (Japanese, Egyptian, Chilean), provided the wife in question comes from the same background as her female readers.

This principle may in fact be applied to any field and is particularly successful with politics. Political topics can be brought to women's notice only if they can be persuaded that the action centers on a woman. The war in Vietnam held female attention only when the press produced the first photos of the legendary Madame Nhu. The problem of Northern Irish Catholics has become interesting to women only since the advent of Bernadette Devlin. No number of articles written about the problems of contemporary Iran helped more toward the understanding of this country than the tragedy of the barren Soraya.

The first political action of any man who seeks power should be marriage to a photogenic woman. One can only guess at the advantages there would have been for Israel or India had Golda Meir or Indira Gandhi been beautiful according to the rigid standards of women. Instead of Grace Kelly or Farah Diba of Iran, their photos would have graced the covers of illustrated magazines. Women would then have read features entitled "The Jewels of Golda Meir," or "Why Indira

Gandhi Appeals to Men"—and as a side effect the other half of the world, i.e., the rich half, would be told again and again about the crisis in Israel, or would realize that in India hundreds of thousands of children are starving to death—children who could easily be saved for the sums of money spent by women on nail polish and nail polish remover.

The Mask of Femininity

THERE IS VIRTUALLY NO DIFFERENCE between an unmade-up, bald, naked woman and an unmade-up, bald, naked man, except their reproductive organs. Any other difference between them is artificially produced. A man becomes a man because he develops his intelligence and, through its development, his productivity. His appearance changes very little. A woman becomes a woman by means of gradual stultification and by deliberately transforming her external appearance, and this differentiation between the sexes is prompted exclusively by women.

As we have said, a man is considered masculine only after a series of manipulations on the part of women. A woman, on the other hand, is the author of her own transformation and produces femininity by means of cosmetics, hair style, and clothes. This femininity, synthetic in origin, consists of two different components: emphasis on secondary sexual characteristics and distancing herself by means of masks. Woman makes use of various types of masks in order to make the difference between herself and a given man as conspicuous as possible.

The first component serves to make her desirable to man, the second to make her mysterious to him. She herself thus creates the equivocal, unknown "opposite sex," making it easier for him to accept his enslavement. Thanks to the wide range of possible transformations each woman can offer a man—and a "real" woman varies her looks just a little every day—she keeps him in a state of constant bewilderment. While he is still trying to find yesterday's woman in today's, she gains time to achieve her own ends. She will maneuver the man into an untenable position, all the time skillfully distracting his attention from the stench of a rotting mind beneath the pleasing mask.

Woman regards her natural self merely as the raw material of a woman. Not the raw material but the end result has to be judged. Unmade-up, without curls and bracelets and necklaces, women are not yet really present. This explains why they do not mind running around in curlers or with cold cream on their faces. It is not "they" at that stage—they are still occupied with the process of becoming "them." They succeed with this sort of make-believe all the more easily because they are not hampered by any kind of intelligence.

No effort is so great that woman will not make it in order to achieve this metamorphosis. No make-up can cost too much, or take too long to put on, when it is a question of the final product which will distinguish them so markedly from men. By rubbing cream into their skins they make them smoother than men's. Their hair is curled or worn long for the same reason. They do not put black mascara around their eyes for the sake of beauty—it is to make their eyes differ from male eyes—strange, mysterious, disturbing.

All this was the original purpose of the female masquerade, but it has almost been forgotten now. In the course of the last few decades, the average middle-class married woman has developed from a rather busy domestic servant into a kind of demimondaine, well padded with the comforts provided by men. As a result of this, her former games, which were for the specific purpose of transforming her appearance, have become an end in themselves. And since amusing themselves with their own bodies is their favorite game, and well-to-do middle-class wives frequently have nothing else to do, they occupy themselves in this way. What is more, they are encouraged to do so by men. After all, it is men who manufacture their cosmetics, design their fashions and hair styles, and make a living by doing so; they do their best to provide these women with new variations, helped by the editors of women's magazines and by women's radio programs. In fact, women have almost succeeded in producing a totally new feminine culture, a sort of women's arts and crafts. In this sanctuary they live among themselves, disturbed by none, being led to heights, or rather into depths, where no man can follow, apart from those specialized slave laborers mentioned above.

"Take care your lips stay smooth," advises, for example, one well-known magazine—this to a woman who complained of badly chapped lips. "Brush your lips daily with a wet toothbrush and use a lip salve with regularity. Never use pearl lipsticks—they settle more easily into the cracks." "Don't forget to take your measurements," the editor goes on to advise all women. "Your pelvic dimensions should never be more than nine inches larger than your waist nor three and a half inches more than your bust." "Always brush your eyebrows into a becoming sweep before outlining them in pencil. And never draw them in with one straight arch. Instead, follow each hair with a separate stroke. It will look completely natural if the lines are vertical nearest the bridge of the nose and carefully toned with two different colors, for instance, gray and brown mixed together." "Always keep a mirror in your kitchen. It will help you to control your face. You will notice if you frown or make faces while you are cooking, or if your hair is in disarray."

Women are grateful for all these rules. They have not enough imagination to think them out for themselves. They follow them religiously, measuring their pelvic dimensions, brushing their lips, outlining their eyebrows, and hanging up little mirrors in the kitchen to avoid wrinkles caused by thinking. And when they have done all that, more fun and games are waiting. There are actually women today who bathe their breasts daily in cold water for ten minutes. "It makes them firm," you see. There are women who oil their bodies all over every morning—and not following medical advice. There are those who twist their hair around thirty-odd curlers every few days and spend at least half an hour making up their eyes. And as they, thanks to all these efforts which, a man feels, are totally absurd anyhow, grow stranger, more incalculable, and more feminine with each passing day, it is often precisely this type of woman who attracts the most willing slaves.

In the meantime, the game goes on. Anyone who wants to join in the game, to keep up with the coterie, has to observe more and more new rules. For women's demands on each other are enormous. Men have long since dropped out of the game. The opportunities for entertainment offered by one's body have increased enormously and will go on doing so though, of course, it is inevitable that many women cannot keep up the pace. These will return to their other source of entertainment: the home.

As the amount of money available to women depends on the husband's income, women are divided into classes. There are those who have an excellent mask, those whose mask is good, and those whose masquerade is merely adequate. The first group become the idols of all the others, and, thanks to the constant efforts of their public-relations organizations, provide a kind of vicarious gratification for them.

Even for a woman with an average type of mask, the rules are getting more and more complicated. If she goes swimming, for example, her make-up must be waterproof, her legs and armpits hairless, her body oiled, and her hair completely hidden by a cap covered with rubber flowers. For the supermarket, a matte base with a dab of rouge and light brown mascara is the thing. Funerals require a pale make-up to enhance the effect of her black lace mantilla and an almost invisible lipstick. For a few minutes at a cocktail party, the preparations of dressing and make-up will take hours. There was a time when only one shade of eye shadow was sufficient. Now it must be three: white, gold, and green, for example. Her lips must be cared for with salves, lip liners, mother-of-pearl lipstick, and powder. False eyelashes, no longer stuck on in one strip, must be carefully gummed in position, one by one. That is "more natural." Her own coiffure must be embellished with an additional hairpiece—and both must always be freshly shampooed and curled. For eye make-up alone the following are basic essentials: false lashes, a special glue, tweezers for putting the lashes in place, mascara, eye liner, three shades of eye shadow, two shades of eyebrow pencil, powder for the brows, plus a specially angled brush for application, a small brush for the eyebrows, oil-based pads for removing the make-up, and special cream to soothe the eyes.

Men adore their women and want them to be divine (exotic, iridescent, that is, *feminine*). At the same time they have no desire to watch their hours of slavish narcissistic primping and are getting more and more uncomfortable. They will never understand the pleasure a woman takes in housework, and to them the make-up process is just as degrading. Every man knows that he himself could not care less if a woman wears three colors of eye shadow or one, just as he knows he has no need of lace curtains or rubber plants in the living room. But he appreciates that other men, or *society,* demand this of a woman, and he feels intensely sorry because he believes himself to be responsible for this degrading state of affairs. Since he realizes that he and the other members of his sex are interested only in woman's external appearance (for what else is there to interest him?), he assumes that his wife's tireless efforts to make herself into an object of desire and to create a certain mystique by means of make-up (which, however, should not be exaggerated) are the signs of an excessive zeal to please him. Of course he feels guilty— and rather touched. Thanks to his primitive needs, he

104

believes that *he* is making woman into this object of his desires; he believes he is suppressing all her worthwhile qualities, which are, in fact, nowhere to be found. As usual he is missing the truth by a hair's breadth. It is in his own interest to deny the fact that this whole development is tantamount to the highest level of feminine culture and that women do not, by means of fashion and cosmetics, make themselves into *objects*, but rather their ceaseless preoccupation with such matters corresponds to the mental activities of infinitely primitive *subjects*.

And there is something else he does not know: a woman does not only re-create herself from day to day, so to speak, getting further and further away from her true self, just for the sake of entertainment. This cult satisfies her minimal need for a religion as well, a need which, as we have already seen, depends on her low level of intelligence. Every step in this process of transformation requires a totally neutral critical observation of self. It forces a woman to regard herself constantly with the eyes of a female stranger, and to test the result of her labors, in terms of that onlooker's eyes, a thousand times a day. If the transformation is a success in those critical eyes, if it passes criticism, she can (still in the eyes of this stranger) indulge in unrestrained self-admiration. Thanks to this trick, she is, as it were, in a position to worship at her own feet, and is therefore to a large extent exempt from every system designed to satisfy a man's pleasure in non-freedom, systems such as ideologies, religions, or glorifications of some other being.

Women are so preoccupied with self and with beautification that men have come to the logical conclusion that, even if women paid any attention to them, they would never be considered handsome. There is an old saying that men do not need to be good-looking: many men will, without *arrière-pensée,* repeat this piece of wisdom. But even if he made an effort, woman would never find man handsome. How could woman, who takes such pleasure in her own ridiculous masquerade, appreciate an unmade-up, conventionally dressed man? What else would this be but the first step, the raw material, the preliminary sketch for a further stage in human development? In a sense this implies that all men must be ugly in woman's eyes—and this frees her to choose according to his income and the standard of living he may be able to offer her.

Particularly sensitive men seem to have realized this recently and are trying to become beautiful according to the standards of women and for once make an impression on them by means of their outward appearance. In the main, however, these attempts to break away from convention have been doomed to failure. In the first place, men could hardly achieve something overnight which women have been cultivating for centuries: man's long hair is never as silky nor his skin as delicate as a woman's. His clothes will never be so exquisitely extravagant. And, in the second place, the vast armies of enslaved men have thrown these deserters out of their ranks and shut them off from earning a proper living.

Today there are few men who wear a mask. Those who do—poets, painters, rock musicians, journalists, actors, hippies, photographers—need just this sort of disguise in order to earn their money, rather as a kind of contemporary court jester. Of course, most of these men have a woman around, someone to put his earnings to immediate use. A poet has his muse, a painter his model, a rock musician his groupie. All of these women live off men. If all men took to growing their hair long, or to wearing chains with pendants around their necks—which, after all, is possible, for every hundred years or so there have been slight changes in men's fashions due to changed working conditions— their long hair would be cut to a uniform length, and those chains around their necks would become a replacement for ties, just as discreet and inconspicuous.

The Business World
as a Hunting Ground

THERE ARE MANY WOMEN who take their place in the working world of today. Secretaries and shop assistants, factory workers and stewardesses—not to mention those countless hearty young women who populate the colleges and universities in ever-increasing numbers. One might even get the impression that woman's nature had undergone a radical change in the last twenty years. Today's young women appear to be less unfair than their mothers. They seem to have decided—perhaps out of pity for their victims—not to exploit men any more, but to become, in truth, their partners.

The impression is deceptive. The only truly important act in any woman's life is the selection of the right partner. In any other choice she can afford to make a mistake. Consequently, she will look for a man where he works or studies and where she can best observe and judge the necessary masculine qualities she values. Offices, factories, colleges, and universities are, to her, nothing but gigantic marriage markets.

The particular field chosen by any young woman as a hunting ground will depend to a large extent on the level of income of the man who has previously been her slave, in other words, her father. The daughters of men in the upper income brackets will choose colleges or universities. These offer the best chances of capturing a man who will earn enough to maintain the standards she has already acquired. Besides, a period of study for form's sake is much more convenient than a temporary employment. Girls from less-well-off homes will have to go into factories, shops, offices, or hospitals for a time—but again with the same purpose in mind. None of them intends to stay in these jobs for long. They will continue only until marriage—or, in cases of hardship, till pregnancy. This offers women one important advantage: any woman who marries nowadays has given up her studies or her job "for the sake of the man of her choice"—and "sacrifices" of this nature create obligations.

Therefore, when women work and study, it merely serves to falsify statistics and furthermore to enslave men more hopelessly than ever, because education and the professions mean something very different when applied to women as opposed to men.

When a man works it is a matter of life and death, and, as a rule, the first years of his life are decisive. Any man of twenty-five who is not well on his way up the ladder can be considered, to all intents and purposes, a hopeless case. At this stage, all his faculties are being developed, and the fight with his competitors is a fight to the death. Behind a mask of business friendship, he is constantly on the watch for any sign of superiority in one of his associates, and he will note its appearance with anxiety. If this same associate shows signs of weakness or indecision, it must be taken advantage of at once. Yet man is only a tiny cog in a gigantic business machine, he himself being in effect exploited at every turn. When he drives others, he drives himself most of all. His orders are really orders from above, passed on by him. If the men at the top occasionally take time to praise him, it is not in order to make him happy: it is only to spur him on, to stimulate him to greater effort. For man, who was brought up to be proud and honorable, every working day is merely an endless series of humiliations. He shows enthusiasm for products he finds useless, he laughs at jokes he finds tasteless, he expresses opinions which are not his own. Not for a moment is he allowed to forget that the merest oversight may mean demotion, that one slip of the tongue may spell the end of his career.

Yet woman, who is the prime cause of all these struggles, and under whose very eyes these fights take place, just stands aside and watches. Going to work means to her flirting and dates, teasing and banter, with the odd bit of "labor" done for the sake of appearances—work for which, as a rule, she has no responsibility. She knows that she is only marking time, and even if she does have to go on working for one reason or another, at least she has had years of pleasant dreams. She watches men's battles from a safe distance, occasionally applauding one of the contestants, encouraging or scolding, and while she makes their coffee, opens their mail, or listens to their telephone conversations, she is cold-bloodedly taking her pick. The moment she has found "Mr. Right," she retires gracefully, leaving the field open to her successors.

The same applies to university education. American colleges admit more and more women, but the percentage who actually complete their courses is less than before the Second World War. They sit happily in lectures designing their spring wardrobe and between classes flirt with the boys. With their scarlet nails carefully protected by transparent rubber gloves, they play around with corpses in the dissecting rooms, while their male colleagues realize their whole future is at stake. If a woman leaves the university with an engagement ring on her finger, she has earned her degree; man has hardly begun when he obtains his diploma. Degrees are, after all, easy to come by—you have only to memorize. How many examiners can tell the difference between real knowledge and bluff? Man, however, has to *understand* his subject as well. His later success will depend on whether his knowledge is well-founded; his

109

later prestige will be built on this, and often other people's lives are dependent on it.

None of these battles exists for woman. If she breaks off her studies and marries a university lecturer, she has achieved the same level as he has without exerting herself. As the wife of a factory owner she is treated with greater respect than he is (and not as somebody who at best would be employable on the assembly line in the same factory). As a wife she always has the same standard of living and social prestige and has to do nothing to maintain them—as he does. For this reason the quickest way to succeed is always to marry a successful man. She does not win him by her industry, ambition, or perseverance—but simply through an attractive appearance.

We have already seen what demands the well-trained man makes on a woman's appearance. The best women trainers—without the least effort—catch the most successful fighters among men. The so-called "beautiful" women are usually those who have had an easy life from their childhood days and therefore have less reason than others to develop their intellectual gifts (intelligence is developed only through competition); it follows as a logical consequence that very successful men usually have abysmally stupid wives (unless, of course, one considers woman's skill at transforming herself into bait for man a feat of intelligence).

It has almost become a commonplace that a really successful man, be he a company director, financier, shipping magnate, or orchestra conductor, will, when he reaches the zenith of his career, marry a beautiful model—usually his second or third wife. Men who have inherited money often take such a supergirl as their first wife—although she will be exchanged over the years for another. Yet, as a rule, models are women of little education who have not even finished school and who have nothing to do until they marry but look beautiful and pose becomingly in front of a camera.

But they are "beautiful"—and that makes them potentially rich.

As soon as a woman has caught her man, she "gives up her career for love"—or, at least, that is what she will tell him. After all, he could hardly be flattered by the thought that she had been saved in the nick of time from having to sweat her way through examinations. He would much rather get drunk on the idea of the love "that knows no compromise," which this woman pretends to feel for him. Who knows, he thinks, she might have become a famous surgeon (celebrated prima ballerina, brilliant journalist), and she has given it all up for him. He would never believe that she preferred to be the wife of a famous surgeon, to have his income and prestige without having either the work or the responsibility. Therefore, he resolves to make her life at his side as comfortable as possible to compensate for her great sacrifice.

A small percentage (ten to twenty percent) of women students in industrial countries of the West do, in fact, obtain their degrees before they get married. Despite occasional exceptions, they are, as a rule, less attractive and have failed to catch a suitable provider while still in school. But then, this degree will automatically raise their market value, for there are certain types of men who feel bolstered if their wife has a degree—providing they have one themselves. It is clear evidence of his own cleverness if such a highly educated woman is interested in him. If by chance this female mastermind happens to be sexy, he will be beside himself with joy.

But not for long. Even women doctors, women sociologists, and women lawyers "sacrifice" their careers for their men, or at least set them aside. They withdraw into suburban ranch houses, have children, plant flower beds, and fill their homes with the usual trash. Within a few years these new entertainments obliterate the small amount of "expert knowledge," learned by rote, of course, and they become exactly like their female neighbors.

The "Emancipated" Female

THERE ARE, HOWEVER, WOMEN who still have jobs or careers at the age of twenty-five or older. There are a variety of reasons for this:

a. The woman is married to a failure. He is not making enough money to provide her with all the useless rubbish she cannot do without.

b. The woman cannot have children. Once the man's passion for her has been spent, he can see no good reason for continuing to support her.

c. The woman is *ugly*.

d. The woman is *emancipated*.

e. The woman is interested in a particular career (and from the start she renounces her own slaves and her own children).

Types (a) and (b) are closely related. It is the next two groups which are important, for an ugly woman is often considered to be emancipated—and this is false. The chance of meeting someone in the last category, a woman who renounces comfort and serfs for intellectual reasons, let alone from a sense of what is fair, is rare indeed.

Let us consider the *ugly* woman. A woman is ugly when she is unattractive to men. That is, when her secondary sexual characteristics are underdeveloped or insufficiently advertised, and because there is an absence in her features of a "baby look." A woman of this type works for the same reason as a man—because there is no one else to do it for her. Yet whereas man keeps a wife and children with his income, she works for herself alone: she would never use the money she earns to finance the life of a beautiful young man.

This type of woman is frequently quite intelligent. True, at the beginning she will have permitted her intellectual capacities to become atrophied because she, like all other women, has been following her mother's example and because she, too, will want to acquire a working slave. But as she gets older, she sees her chances dwindle, and one day she finds herself faced with the fact that there is nothing else for her to do but remember and resurrect the last remnants of what was once her mind, and make the best of it.

Some women in this group achieve a very real success. They frequently obtain high honors (simply because they are unusual, a rare species, these intellectual women), and they are often journalists, authors, politicians, doctors, or lawyers. What is more, they render a great service to the exploiters in the suburban ranch houses. "Look at that," these women say. "We could do as well, but we renounced it all for you." The man, put off by these few examples of intelligent womanhood, is only too glad to cling to his imbecile, who will tell him that those "intellectual" bluestockings are ugly, bitter, lacking in charm, in sum, "unwomanly." And his preference for the lobotomized creature lying in his bed will increase a thousandfold: after all, if necessary, if he becomes really desperate, he can always find a man to talk to.

Not even an ugly woman, despite her success, ever wants to give up her special feminine status entirely. She seems to take it for granted that the world should admire her as a kind of eighth wonder of the world—a woman who has actually achieved personal success. She will emphasize her "femininity" in every possible way until it becomes almost obscene. She will appear on television and give interviews to the press whenever possible, her flabby bosom hanging over her large desk, complaining how hard it is for her, as a woman, to maintain her status in a man's world.

Be that as it may, she is, compared to the usual female exploiter, comparatively respectable and honest. The fact that this honesty has been forced upon her (and you have only to look at her face to realize why she is so successful) is another matter altogether. There is no virtue in ugliness.

Things become rather more complicated when one comes to consider the case of the so-called "emancipated" woman. The first three categories of women can easily be tempted away from their work by bribery—and this includes the ugly woman (before she has become successful). An emancipated woman, however, never works for money. She must by definition have been attractive even as a young girl and therefore have had slaves with good incomes at hand. Therefore, it is only the "beautiful" woman who *can* become "emancipated." An ugly woman, like a man, is never in this position. No one has ever attempted to corrupt her. Since she, again like men, has nothing to emancipate herself from, she has no choice but to work.

The emancipated woman has all the accessories of the average housewife: a comfortable apartment, the necessary status symbols of her coterie, and children (seldom more than one or two, though). The difference lies in the fact that her sphere of entertainment is not limited to the home or the masquerades given by her own sex. She entertains herself best by undertaking some inferior form of drudgery where she is surrounded by a fairly large audience. We find her wandering airily along the corridors of publishing houses and newspaper offices; we meet her in the anterooms of film producers, television executives, and theatrical managers; she is a production assistant or an interpreter. She will be found behind the counter of a travel agency, in a jeweler's, an antique dealer's, or a boutique. In fact, anywhere where she can meet rich and interesting people. And her money? That is spent almost entirely on her elaborate masks, which keep her with-it and up-to-date at her place of work.

In fact, the emancipated woman is just as stupid as the others, but she does not want people to think so. If she mentions housewives, it is with utter contempt. As she has a job which would not be unworthy of a man, she believes that this very fact alone makes her intelligent, but she is confusing cause and effect. Men work only because they have to and not because they are intelligent. Most men would start to make proper use of their intelligence if they were free of financial obligations, as free as housewives, for example. A woman living at home has, in fact, far better opportunities of enjoying a stimulating, intellectual life than one who is stuck between typewriter and dictaphone.

The work chosen by an emancipated woman rarely involves effort or responsibility, although she makes herself believe it involves both. As far as she is concerned, "it is satisfying," "stimulating," and "keeps her from stagnating." She "simply couldn't exist without it." Yet if one gets down to the facts, she is never really dependent on it. Unlike the ugly woman, she could give it up any time. She never works without life-saving apparatus. The moment there is any sign of difficulty on the horizon, up jumps a man from somewhere in the wings and rushes to her aid.

This type of woman finds it unfair that she does not get on as fast as a man, but on the other hand she never allows herself to become part of the murderous rat race. The complaint she utters is always the same: even as an emancipated woman, one simply is not given the same chances as a man. Instead of fighting for her chance on the spot, she runs off, covered in make-up like a clown and looking like a Christmas tree, to yell for women's rights and women's equality at one of the meetings held by her coterie. It would never occur to her that she alone, and not man, is the cause of this unequal state of affairs—she, woman, with her total lack of interest, her stupidity, her venality, her unreliability, her ridiculous masquerades, and her eternal pregnancies, and, above all, because of her merciless manipulation of man. How could *she* have caused the situation?

On the other hand, men may well think that the husbands of emancipated women are lucky: they do not have to bear the financial responsibilities alone. The contrary is the case: the husbands of so-called emancipated women are usually extremely unhappy. After all, they have had the same basic training as other men, and so they are always trying to keep one step ahead of their wives. A translator's husband will be a writer, a shorthand typist's a departmental manager, a pottery maker's a sculptor, a feature writer's an editor. Therefore, an emancipated woman is far from being a help to her man. She exploits him even more than the others. The higher she rises, the more relentlessly she drives him. Such women, either by chance or because they are attractive enough to be protected by some man, often rise to really important positions. If his position is comparatively low, every time she gets an increase of salary it will be a traumatic experience for him. Professional recognition of her will merely put him in a panic. He lives in a constant fear that one day she will overtake him, and, on top of it, he suffers agonies of jealousy about the strange men she meets every day. He feels superfluous, and his whole existence seems pointless because she no longer seems to need him. The one true happiness of the slave—the only happiness left to manipulated man—is now denied him.

A woman of this type does not even make her children happy. After all, she is only different from other women, not better. She is entertained more by her stupid office work than by her children. But she is not going to give up having them. A woman, she will say, has to experience motherhood, otherwise she will not be "fulfilled."

In fact, this woman has her cake and eats it too. She does not want to give up her "stimulating mental work" and is able to bundle her children off to nurseries or boarding schools or to leave them in the care of one of those much despised housewives. She does not even do the housework. That is shared by her husband after office hours. While he waxes the floors, waters the plants, and polishes the silver, he is meant to carry on stimulating intellectual conversation with her. For the emancipated woman renounces neither the traditional rubbish of her clique, nor her work slave and children.

In order to emphasize her claims to masculine prerogatives, her claim, that is, to the highly paid positions of men and not to the "prerogatives" of, say, soldiers, emancipated women from time to time organize so-called "movements." Such campaigns give her an opportunity to draw the world's attention to her with a great deal of shouting and noise, to wear badges and dress up in the latest suffragette look, and to openly demonstrate her political views by putting lighted candles in her living-room windows. In full view of the television public, women have pinched the bottoms of building-site workers and perpetrated other absurdities. Woman frees herself from her imaginary "chains" at regular intervals: spiritual ones being unknown to her, she interprets them literally. At the turn of the century it was the corset that went. In the seventies the bra, and just to make sure that everyone knew about it, she got men to make see-through blouses. Perhaps in the next wave of emancipation it will the uncomfortable long skirt which goes—the skirt they have just flirtatiously readopted and made part of their props, despite general male disapproval. But their stupidity, their inanity, their ridiculous behavior, their mendacity and lack of feeling, and their tedious and abysmally stupid chatter are still there: women have never taken any steps to get rid of those.

No matter how much a woman is earning, she will never let a man take her place in the house, nor will she take on his responsibility for earning their livelihood or maintaining their social prestige. Even though it is quite possible—since she is much more thick-skinned and consequently will suffer less by doing work of deadly routine—that a job really does "fulfill" her and make her "happy," she will never help *him* with *her* money. She will never open doors for him or light his cigarette; she will never take out any insurance policy in his favor or give him alimony should there be a divorce— that is not considered "feminine." Neither would it occur to a man to expect such a settlement—he has been conditioned too well. The husband of the emancipated woman will simply give his wife a kiss, wipe the traces of face cream, powder, and lipstick from his face, and throw himself once again into the battle.

American Man—
the Most Successfully
Manipulated Male on Earth

THE EXPLOITATION OF THE AMERICAN MALE by the American female would be a purely American affair were it not a model for women all over the world. Unfortunately, the economic hegemony of the U.S.A. influences not just the politics, science, research, and culture of all other capitalist countries but, to a great extent, the social behavior of their populations. Through the mass media, which have been relentlessly perfected, this influence spreads to all areas of life more and more rapidly. The old maxim about American consciousness becoming the consciousness of the world after a five-year lag no longer holds true. Modern techniques of communication have flooded over the boundaries separating place and time. If the United States develops a new treatment for heart attacks, hospitals in Latin America will be using that very treatment a few weeks later. If the performance of American schoolchildren is improved by teaching machines, these same machines will be hooked up within a short time in the classrooms of Japan. The moment a hit like *Jesus Christ Superstar* opens on Broadway, students in West Germany start praying. As soon as the American female compares her situation with that of American blacks, women in England, France, and Scandinavia scream, "We are the Niggers of the Nation."

While American influence has its benefits in other spheres (for example, in research), in the social sphere, as far as the social position of men in these countries is concerned, surely there is none. There is no country in which men are worse off than they are in the United States. They are worse off by comparison with their female partners—and this is what we are discussing here: the differing living conditions of man and woman within one and the same social class of a given country, within one and the same family.

Nobody will deny that the struggle of a poor white-collar worker to survive is more difficult in Portugal than in Sweden and that in the same country a factory worker's wife has a harder life than the wife of an engineer. These injustices are the subject of many other books; here we can discard them entirely. By comparison with her husband—not by comparison with the engineer's wife—the factory worker's wife leads a luxurious life.

America's high standard of living, combined with its permanent threat of unemployment, is enough to make any man's life miserable. In no country with a comparable standard of living are jobs so tenuous; in no other country with a comparable rate of unemployment are the demands made by the standard of living as high. The difference between a "success" and a "failure" is nowhere so clearly defined as in the U.S.A. Added to these external difficulties is the fact that no other man is so thoroughly manipulated as the American male. The adult American male is manipulated so expertly that there appears to be nothing he would not willingly endure. And, indeed, he is exploited without scruple. In no other country do mothers so pitilessly train the male infant to perform. No other society exists where the male sexual drive is exploited for money so unscrupulously. Nobody except the American woman so shamelessly professes a creed of profit under the guise of love.

This does not mean that American women are cruel. Women are never cruel to their men; men are usually not important enough to be tortured. Only in movies do women ruin their men *intentionally*. This simply means that American women, more than other women, fail to consider men as fellow human beings. Perhaps the many dangers of pioneering days caused American men to be evaluated by their usefulness to women. After all, that period in history is not that far gone.

And American men prefer to see themselves in this role: a man's salary is the yardstick of his worth. America is the only place where a badly paid professor is a bad professor, and an unsuccessful writer a bad writer. For the Latin American male, masculinity is still associated with sexual potency. For the American male, however, the association is directly with money. American literature, from Edward Albee to Jacqueline Susann, revolves around this question: whether or not a male is a man if he cannot provide appropriately for the woman in his life. Of course he is not.

The American man knows: happiness comes only through women, and women are expensive. He is ready to pay that price. As a young adult he pays in advance, as a grownup he pays in installments, and as a corpse he is cashed in for a fortune. A man from another country realizes this as soon as he sees a flourishing divorce paradise like Reno, or the thousands of his fellow men sitting in jail for overdue alimony payments. On the other hand, the American man views this as confirmation of his superiority. Is he not the privileged one, as he has enough money to pay for it all? Is he not the competent one, since he goes to work? Would his wife have taken on his family and surname were he not the master? Only recently a poll showed that more American men than women believe that women are suppressed, and fifty-one percent of American men believe that the situation of the American white woman is as bad as that of the American black man.

The American man is grateful to his wife for letting him go to work, because work to him is a male privilege. The woman for whom he provides has made sure that he never doubts it, and he feels sorry for her in spite of the unequivocal difference between his situation and hers. She has made sure that he sees a sacrifice in her waiver of work. He, more than any other man, mistakes his wife's lack of intellectual ambition for modesty, her stupidity for exceptional femininity, her giving up responsibilities for love. More than any other man, he is able to close his eyes to the clear evidence of his own exploitation.

In this country man is manipulated with much less inhibition than in other countries: hence women should be even easier to unmask. But the American man does not want to see or know. It seems appropriate to him that in the TV show his children are watching, the father is portrayed as a fool, the mother as a star. Wasn't his own mother superb? That a Mafia of women's groups controls all cultural life seems unavoidable to him. Somebody has to take care of culture. That American women (and no other women in the rest of the world) run around in public with curlers in their hair is charming American folklore to him. The fact that a majority of psychiatric patients are women, while men have a higher rate of suicide, is his evidence for the value of psychoanalysis. He thinks it fair that for generations men have become crippled war veterans, while generations of women do not even know what a hand grenade looks like. Man is stronger and the stronger one goes to war.

Though the slavery of the American man is humiliating and nerve-racking, he does not want to see, of course, that his is the worst bargain: he has ended up with the most made-up, constantly recolored, the most conspicuously masked woman of all, in short, with the most unreal woman. But to this he closes his eyes.

Since the American woman is the highest paid wife, she, of course, wants something in return for her money. She is the leading consumer of cosmetics: she uses more lipstick, more cream, more powder, more color than a woman of any other nationality. Although she has a reputation for being especially dowdy, she needs more money for her clothes and other masquerades.

Of all women, she leads the most comfortable life. More often than her sisters of other nationalities, she lives in her own house, drives her own car, goes on vacation, does her work with the help of machines, and uses ready-to-cook food. She has a fully automated household, a bus takes her children to school, and they are gone almost all day, so that she has every opportunity to go to work; and yet the percentage of married women working in America is considerably lower than in other industrialized countries. Although the American woman has a better chance at a higher education than women of other countries, and although she is spared two years of military service, only thirteen percent of American coeds get their university degrees.

America has the highest divorce rate, and the chance that an infant will grow up with both a mother *and* a father is slimmer than in any other country. But that does not seem to disturb the American woman, for out of all women of highly industrialized nations, she has the highest birth rate. No wonder; children are a guarantee of income. American fathers pay the highest alimonies, and since non-payment can be punished by imprisonment, he pays promptly.

Even his old-age insurance rates are the highest. The average American husband is four years older than his wife, and his average life expectancy is seven years less than hers. The eleven years by which she will probably survive him do not represent a risk, and if she clings to her husband for life, she will be respected and well treated because of her money, so that the years will be even more comfortable without him. She plays bridge,

123

is active in sports, has visits from her children and grandchildren, and works in her women's groups for law and order. In flowery hats, her withered lips painted Stoplight Red (look, here comes an American woman!), she takes off once in a while for a tour around the world and makes sure that she is not forgotten abroad. And she is not; on the contrary: when an aging Rose Kennedy (having already sacrificed to her nation three male heirs while daughters and daughters-in-law are getting rich and old in the process) flirts in front of TV cameras, hoping to promote her last living son's campaign for the presidency, she is celebrated as a heroine. What a brave mother!

One might assume that a prerequisite for the high profit achieved by American woman's femininity would be top performance in other areas. But for the connoisseur, she is neither a good cook nor an experienced lover. Despite her good salary, the demands on her art of seduction are minimal. Her husband, trained by Hollywood to appreciate the coarsest of sex symbols (large breasts and big behinds), can no longer make fine distinctions. All she really needs are a few good curves and the nerve to say no long enough. And she is a true master of that art. Necking and petting are an American invention. To lure men, like the women of other countries they wear false breasts, but only in America are false bottoms worn.

The logical result of such business tactics, steadily perfected through the generations, is frigidity, and the American woman has succeeded in persuading the nation that her frigidity is an illness to be taken seriously. After all, there is a difference: a prostitute would be willing to give up her orgasm, a wife would not. Instead of asking what a frigid woman is doing in the bed of a man, a man she does not even desire, an attempt is made to free her from her suffering through costly procedures and with ever-changing prescriptions (it goes without saying: only if she is properly married. Before

124

marriage, she would have had neither the money for therapy nor the interest in getting better).

The American woman is no worse than other women. She is only ahead of them all. Her unscrupulous tactics for exploitation would not be so dangerous if they were not constantly idealized by a powerful TV and film industry. As the latter creates the image of Western woman, her behavior is being copied, and as her standard of living is constantly raised, the fate of her husband automatically becomes the fate of men in other countries. Yet there is another reason to deal specifically with the American woman, and that is Women's Liberation. American women are better off than other women around the world: but not all of the American women. The same system that brings so many advantages to most American women turns by necessity against a minority within their own ranks: the women who are unattractive by male standards.

Until recently, this condition went unnoticed by all save that minority. But one day this minority decided not to put up with that condition any longer and began to organize, like their predecessors, the suffragettes. Since the American public is accustomed to listening to women when they talk, their problems were soon much discussed. Not only in America but in the rest of the world, this new movement was taken up immediately. Why, one might ask, did this uprising of women start in America, of all places, where women are obviously better off? The explanation is simple: exactly for that reason. Because the American woman is better off, because social differences between married women and women who earn their own living are so enormous. Because in America more than any other country the working woman is treated as a traitor, an outcast, by the masses of female exploiters who see their own interests betrayed. This is why this movement had to start in the U.S.A. and no other place. Used to endless power over man and to the highest social prestige, American women will find the renunciation of power and prestige much more painful. And if the direct approach will not work, she will procure her insignia of feminine power in a roundabout way: Women's Liberation.

Furthermore, a strained labor market has put this minority of women, forced or willing to work, into a somewhat more difficult position than their European sisters when they apply for higher positions. Many of them will see their difficulties from a particular perspective and interpret the unpleasantness of professional life as discrimination against their sex. But if an American employer were to fill an open position and to choose between an unattractive woman who did not appeal to his sexual instinct and a man, his choice would undoubtedly be the man. And he can even justify that decision: when a woman marries, she will give up her job as soon as she becomes a mother. A man who marries and becomes a father turns into an even more reliable employee. If the applicant is already married, then the employer's choice is even easier, since he knows that the man's paycheck will almost certainly support more than one person, hence be twice as necessary. The single woman supports, at most, herself. From the employer's point of view, it is more humane to give the job to the man. The "woman with a family"—*the woman who supports a healthy man and his children all her life*—is practically unknown in the professional world. Who should be held responsible for this situation: employer or woman?

It is at once sad and comic to see how the women of the American Women's Liberation movement, who indeed have reason to fight, direct all their time and energy against the wrong enemy. With constant defamations, they hold their only allies, men, at bay, while spoiling the really guilty party with immoderate compliments. Like all women's liberating movements in history, Women's Liberation started from the wrong premise and has missed its aim. But no force on earth will convince its members of that.

The responsibility lies with the intellectuals. It is understandable and perhaps even forgivable that, as a result of all the manipulation from earliest childhood, men have come to the conclusion that (a) they have the power, and (b) they will use it to suppress women.

But it is inexcusable that intellectual women, who might have seen matters from a very different (female) angle, have uncritically adopted this line of thought. Instead of saying, "It is very nice of you to think so highly of us, but in reality we are quite different from the way you see us, we do not deserve your pity and your compliments at all," they say, "With all due respect to your insight, we are much more pitiable, suppressed, and exploited than your male brains could ever imagine!" These intellectual women have claimed a rather dubious fame for their sex: instead of being unmasked as the most cunning slave traders in history, they have undersold women and made them the object of male charity: man the tyrant, woman the victim. Men are flattered, of course. Part of their manipulation has trained them to interpret the word "tyrant" as a compliment. And they accept this female definition of woman happily. It very closely matches their own.

Even Simone de Beauvoir let this opportunity pass when she wrote her book *The Second Sex* (1949), which could have been the first book on the subject of women. Instead she created a handbook of Freud's, Marx's, Kant's, etc., ideas about women. Rather than looking for once at woman, she researched the books men had written and found, of course, signs of woman's disadvantage everywhere. The novelty of her work lay in the fact that for the first time, men's opinion of women carried the signature of a woman. But now the way was clear: Betty Friedan, Kate Millett, Germaine Greer ... each a repetition of the last; they went head over heels in their effort to come up with evidence of male infamy. But they wrote nothing really worth mentioning on their subject: women. They copied the male idea about women, without being aware that this idea can only be the result of female manipulation, and thus they became, by imitating men, the victims of their own (female) system.

Nothing has changed since, although women today, more than ever before, have every opportunity to make statements about themselves on their own radio or TV programs, in newspaper columns or magazines. But they do nothing except repeat and chew over the old mothballed ideas men have about women, adding new details here and there. Instead of pointing out to their following what a miserable lot they really are, the peak of female dignity is achieved by rejecting advertising for bras or vaginal sprays. The peak of female originality is reached the moment a women's magazine carries a male nude centerfold à la *Playboy*.

These are the reasons why yet another Women's Liberation movement has failed: the enemies they fought were really friends, and the real enemy remained undetected. Once again the fixed idea of sexual solidarity (under the circumstances a solidarity with a syndicate at best) misled women to the wrong strategy. And they were not aware of it. Their struggle was aided almost exclusively by men. But since they live under the delusion that they are persecuted by men, they mistook the flexibility of men for a sign of female strength and screamed that much louder. And nobody got offended. From *The New York Times* to *The Christian Science Monitor,* from *Playboy* to *Newsweek,* from Kissinger to McGovern, everybody was for Women's Liberation. No marches of men were organized against them, nobody prevented their demonstrations. And none of them were taken to task for their unending defamation of men, a Senator Joe McCarthy oppressing Women's Liberation was missing, the F.B.I. did not lift a finger against them.

Just as their predecessors, the suffragettes, secured the right to vote for women withing a short period (a right they left unused by not electing women to political power and by not stopping war), Women's Liberation saw most of their demands fulfilled immediately. The outrageous inequities in the law had, after all, been established by men for women's protection. But the ladies themselves did not see it that way, and, when they insisted on change, within months they succeeded. The right of a waitress to work night shifts, the right of a woman mechanic to carry heavy-duty equipment, the right to mount telephone poles, the right to pay alimony to men, the right to use her own surname and with that the right for a wife to act as a solely responsible legal person, the right to military service, the right to fight in war, etc.—they have them all. Infected by this wave of general generosity, even the government did not want to be left behind: In the future, it proclaimed, government contracts will be given out to only those companies who do not discriminate against women willing to work.

But the army of suppressed women eagerly awaiting that moment of liberation simply never materialized. As soon as the first American woman had climbed a telephone pole; the first female plumber, construction worker, and furniture mover had been photographed and the photos printed in newspapers all over the world; the uproar died down. Why should it have gone any further? After all, it is not much fun to repair water pipes, to lay bricks, or to lug furniture. Unlike men, women can choose whether they want to do drudgery or not. It is logical that most of them decide against it. And given a choice, they will also avoid military service and going to war. Women think of themselves as pacifists: wars are started by men, despite women's right to vote.

Left in the lurch by their own sex, the theorists among Women's Liberationists further entangled themselves in details: can every sexual intercourse with a man be considered an assault? Should a vaginal orgasm be accepted at all? Is the lesbian the only truly emancipated woman? Is the woman question more urgent than the racial question? And so on. Enticed by the extensive publicity awaiting them, a number of attractive "emancipated" women joined the movement. (Where else does a pretty woman attract more attention than among ugly ones?) And although these attractive women could not possibly imagine themselves having the problems they were discussing (discrimination against an attractive woman does not exist, either in her profession or in her private life), they soon took on leading roles within the movement and turned it more and more into a branch of American show business, and—as defined in the previous chapter—into a "genuine" movement for emancipation.

Meanwhile, the exploiters living in the suburbs started to organize. The Liberationists' loud demands for work, and the men who were willing to gratify these demands, unintentionally put the suburban ladies into a most embarrassing situation. In organizations such as Man Our Masters and Pussycat League, they assured the world how wrong the aims of Women's Liberation really are and how much happiness a woman can find in the service of her husband and children.

The most curious of all countermovements came from a faction within Women's Liberation itself: "We don't want men's jobs," these women protested. "If all women start to work now, we will soon have an economic crisis. What we want is not to be degraded as eunuchs any longer, we want to evolve freely, and we don't want man to suppress our intellectual development and our sexual drive anymore."

This argument is curious not only because woman now holds man responsible also for her crippled sexual drive (he who likes nothing better than a woman who thinks sex is fun). It also makes obvious for the first time how foreign it is to a woman to think that *she* could support her family. It would never occur to her that women do not necessarily cause an economic crisis when they enter a profession. Working women would not necessarily increase the absolute number of employed persons within their community. Whether women can work does not have to depend on the existence of day-care centers, since the quality of child care does not depend on the sex of the person administering it. Fathers could manage that work as well.

But for a woman work has to be *fun,* and to make sure it is, the employed wife needs a working husband. If she goes to work, she might as well make some demands, and one of these demands will be that she can choose her work and quit any time she feels like it. So she brings her newborn child to a day-care center rather than lose her working partner, and before her profession can turn into an obligation and responsibility, she quits, rather than allow her husband to stay home in her place.

Women's Liberation has failed. The story of the underprivileged woman was an invention—and against an invention one cannot stage a rebellion. Once again, men are the mourners. In a country where man is exploited as unscrupulously by women as in the U.S.A., a movement that fights for yet more of women's rights is reactionary, and, as long as the screaming for female equality does not stop, man will never get the idea that he is actually the victim.

Even the emancipation of women has not been attained. "Liberation of women" would mean her abdication from the privileges she now has. It was Women's Liberation that made sure that this would never happen.

"It's better to let them think they are king of the castle," a female reader of *Psychology Today* wrote, "lean and depend on them, and continue to control and manipulate them as we always have."

What Is Love?

MAN HAS BEEN MANIPULATED by woman to the point where he cannot live without her and therefore will do anything she asks of him. He fights for his life and calls it *love*. There are even men who will threaten their idolized female with suicide unless she accepts him. Not that this is much of a risk for them—they have nothing to lose.

Woman, nevertheless, is incapable of living without man. Like a queen bee, she cannot survive on her own. She, too, is fighting for her life, and she, too, calls it *love*. They each need one another, in fact, and it seems therefore that they share at least *one* sentiment. The cause, nature, and consequences of this sentiment, however, differ as much as do the sexes.

To a woman love means power, to a man enslavement. Love provides woman with an excuse for financial exploitation, man with an emotionally charged excuse. "For the sake of love" woman will do things that are of advantage only to herself, while man does only those things that will harm him. When a woman marries, she gives up her career "for the sake of love." When a man marries, he will have to work for two "for the sake of love." For both sexes, love is a fight for survival. But the one survives only by being victorious, the other only by being defeated. It is a paradox that women can also make their greatest gains during moments of utter passivity and that the word "love" endows them with a halo of selflessness, even at the moment of their most pitiless deception of man.

As a result of "love," man is able to hide his cowardly self-deception behind a smoke screen of sentiment. He is able to make himself believe that his senseless enslavement to woman and her hostages is more than an act of honor, it has a higher purpose. He is entirely happy in his role as a slave and has arrived at the goal he has so long desired. Since woman gains nothing but one advantage after another from the situation as it stands today, things will never change. The system forces her to be corrupt, but no one is going to worry about that. Since one can expect nothing from a woman but *love,* it will remain the currency for any need she might have. Man, her slave, will continue to use his energies only according to his conditioning and never to his own advantage. He will achieve greater goals, and the more he achieves, the farther women will become alienated from him. The more he tries to ingratiate himself with her, the more demanding she will become; the more he desires her, the less she will find him desirable; the more comforts he provides for her, the more indolent, stupid, and inhuman she will become—and man will grow lonelier as a result.

Only woman can break the vicious circle of man's manipulation and exploitation—but she will not do it. There is absolutely no compelling reason why she should. It is useless to appeal to her feelings, for she is callous and knows no pity. And so the world will go on, sinking deeper and deeper into this morass of kitsch, barbarism, and inanity called *femininity*. And man, that wonderful dreamer, will never awaken from his dream.

ABOUT THE AUTHOR

ESTHER VILAR was born in 1935 of German parents in Buenos Aires, Argentina. She was trained as a physician and in 1960 went to West Germany to continue her studies in psychology and sociology. She worked as a staff doctor in a Bavarian hospital for a year, and has also been a translator, a saleswoman, an assembly-line worker in a thermometer factory, a shoe model, and a secretary. She was married to German author Klaus Wagn for two years and they have a seven-year-old son.

READ THE WOMEN
WHO TAKE STANDS
AND ACT ON THEM

WE DELIVER!
And So Do These Bestsellers.